Best pub walks
in north pembrokeshire

best pub walks
in
north
pembrokeshire

Paul Williams

ISBN: 978–1-84524-188-9

Cover design: Lynwen Jones

First edition: 2012
Llygad Gwalch, Ysgubor Plas, Llwyndyrys,
☎: 01758 750432   🖷: 01758 750438
🖰: lona@carreg-gwalch.com
Website: www.carreg-gwalch.com

contents

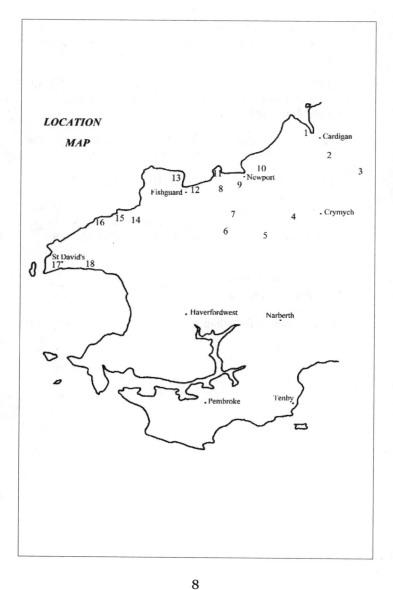

LOCATION
MAP

1

. Cardigan

2

3

10
. Newport

13

8   9

Fishguard .   12

. Crymych

7

4

16   15   14

6

5

St David's
17 .   18

. Haverfordwest   Narberth

. Pembroke   Tenby .

Introduction

Out and About

Those familiar with my *Circular Walks in North Pembrokeshire* will find fourteen new walks in this

volume, however the four old favourites are well worth repeating! All walks are easy to follow, and clear directions are given. The exact location for the starting point of each walk is noted, and how to get there. Relevant bus routes and numbers are included – though given that Pembrokeshire is a rural area services can be infrequent. Nor do all buses operate on Sundays. Train services are also listed. Check with Information Centres for full details. The County Council with contributions from the National Park operate summer Coastal bus services to the more popular coastal areas, and their popularity has led to them continuing to operate three days a week through the winter months. There is adequate parking space at the start of each walk – precise details are given.

Walks vary in length from 3 miles/4.75 kilometres to 9 miles/14.5 kilometres. The routes utilise the long distance Pembrokeshire Coast Path, public footpaths, bridleways and the occasional permissive path, as at Porth Clais. They are well maintained, and clearly

9

signposted and waymarked – a yellow arrow or waymark indicating a public footpath, a blue one a bridleway. As many stiles as is practicable are being replaced with gates, making access for the less able easier. An acorn indicates the route is a long distance path, and is often confused with the, quite separate, National Trust's logo of an oak leaf. Many people are uncertain of how long a walk of, for example, 7 miles would take. As a rough guide an average walker would expect to cover 3 miles/4.75 kilometres an hour over level ground, on the ascent an hour for every 2000 feet/600 metres. Sketch maps for each walk are provided – but the author advises that the local Ordnance Survey (OS) 1:25 000 are used alongside these. The 1:50 000 series (1.25 inches = 1 mile/2 centimetres = 1 kilometre) cover the county in three maps: Cardigan, St David's and Haverfordwest, and Tenby. Those preferring greater detail will wish to acquire the Outdoor Leisure and Explorer 1:25 000 series (2.5 inches = 1 mile/4 centimetres = 1 kilometre). The yellow covered Outdoor Leisure series covers the majority of the county in two maps: 35 North Pembrokeshire and 36 South Pembrokeshire. The majority of walks in this guide will be found on the 35 North Pembrokeshire map; one and half of one other on the Explorer 185 Newcastle Emlyn/Castell Newydd Emlyn map. Much has been said of the recent 'right to roam', the Right of Access on foot to large areas of Wales given by the introduction in 2005 of the Countryside and Rights of Way (CROW) Act. In practice this means a right to walk on open county ie moor, mountain, heath and down, and on registered common land. This 'Access Land' (see OS maps) makes up about 10% of the National Park, largely in the north of the county. It does not apply to built up areas, farmyards, field and woodland, where public paths only can be utilised.

The grading system used is largely self-explanatory. Easy walks involve short walks over easy terrain, with little variation in contour. Moderate may have one or two short steep sections, with a little more variety in landscape. The author stresses that the term 'easy' and 'moderate' are used by comparison to 'challenging' and 'strenuous' – all walks can have their problems and please heed the notice on page 45. History notes are included which are designed to give both a historical note of the pubs featured on the walk, as well as a quick snapshot of the particular area, what gives a place in landscape or historical terms it's own brand of uniqueness. Many Pembrokeshire pubs close in the afternoons, so check opening times if required; phone numbers of all pubs are listed. Most provide food, and many welcome children, and will allow dogs. Some offer accommodation. As all but one of the walks are circular they may be joined at any convenient point, (or either end in the case of the linear one!), and details of parking at the most accessible points are listed under a number of the walks. Included under facilities are the nearest BT telephones, public toilets, cafes, Post Offices and shops, youth hostels, caravan sites etc. Most small towns and many farms will offer B&B – check with Information Centres if you are interested. Also listed under facilities are any additional places of interest in the neighbourhood, for example gardens and garden centres.

Finally a word of warning caution. Footpaths get muddy, the foreshore can get slippery, and cliffs can be dangerous. Take care! Ensure you have adequate clothing, and the proper footwear, ie boots or stout shoes, for each walk. Follow the Country Code!

lanɖscape anɖ cultuʀe

Pembrokeshire – the name is an Anglicisation of the Welsh *Pen Fro*, or Land's End – juts out into the sea at the south west corner of Wales. Surrounded on three sides by the powerhouses of the Atlantic Ocean and the Irish Sea it's spectacular cliffs are studded with glittering coves and bays. One of the essential features of the landscape is its many isolated peninsulas; another the extraordinary flatness of the land. Only the heather clad hills of Preseli (home of the bluestones of Stonehenge), the great stone outcrops at Strumble Head, St David's and Treffgarne gorge, and the southern Ridgeway, rise above the uniformity. In the south, like a sword slash, the Milford Haven tears the plateau apart. The county is renowned for it's magnificent coast and it's sandy shores, yet it has a magic and uniqueness which goes beyond these, for it is a microcosm of the major habitats to be found in Britain. The coastal waters are particularly rich in marine flora and fauna; the Pembrokeshire islands and coast, and the Milford Haven waterway, being designated as the Pembrokeshire Marine Special Area of Conservation (SAC) in December 2004. The coast plays host to some five thousand grey seals;

harbour porpoises and bottlenose dolphins are common sitings. The bird islands of Grassholm, Skomer and Skokholm are of international importance. Grassholm is one of the world's largest gannetries, Skomer probably the planet's top spot for the Manx

Skomer puffins

shearwater. Home to razorbills and guillemots, fulmars, kittiwakes and puffins the islands are not to be missed. Good mainland locations for birdwatchers are, in the north of the county, at Dinas Head and Strumble Head, and, in the south, near Bosherston, at Stack Rocks and Stackpole Head.

Pembrokeshire's cliffs, at their highest in the north, are regal in spring and early summer. Magical yellows of gorse and bird's-foot trefoil mingle with the pinks of the thrift and the whites of sea campion. The succession of flowers continues, as if to an ordered floral banquet, from March to August. In the south are the main sand dune systems, extensive at Penally and Freshwater West, with smaller systems at Broad Haven South and Manorbier. Northern systems, some protected, are at Whitesands Bay, Newport and Poppit Sands. Sheltered behind shingle banks or sand bars are pockets of saltmarsh. Usually found at the mouths of estuaries they are hostile to all but the most salt tolerant plants. The Gann, at Pickleridge near Dale, is perhaps the most important, with others at Newport and the Teifi river at

Cardigan. Together with intertidal mudflats, formed by the accumulation of silt where fresh and salt waters meet, they are highly important feeding grounds for thousands of overwintering waders and wildfowl. The mudflats of Angle Bay, in the south of the county, and the western and eastern arms of the Cleddau river, are particularly popular.

Freshwater habitats include the marshes found at the flood plains of rivers and streams. Good examples are at Penally, and at Pentood marsh in Cilgerran Wildlife Centre. The largest area of open water in the National Park are the delightful lily ponds at Bosherston, a highly popular summer venue. Llys y Frân Reservoir and Country Park, opened in the 1970s, attracts a number of winter waterfowl, as well as offering water sports and fishing. Remnants of the oak forest which once covered Pembrokeshire remain. Clinging to the sides of isolated valleys and hills, and along the steeper sections of rivers, they have a unique beauty and atmosphere. Cwm Gwaun in it's summer yellows and greens, or with the early morning winter mist rising from the water, is rightly famous, whilst hidden amongst the steep oak woods of the Cleddau are Norman river castles; whitewashed Benton opposite Lawrenny, or Carew, glimpsed through the trees bordering the Carew river. The Gwaun valley woodlands, together with the National Nature Reserves of Tŷ Canol and Pengelli Forest near Felindre Farchog, have been designated the North Pembrokeshire Woodlands Special Area of Conservation (SAC). Less dramatic are the uniform stands of coniferous plantations which dot the uplands.

In the north of the county are the Preseli hills, extensive areas of lowland heath, acid grassland and moorland. They are predominantly heath, dominated by heather, with gorse in western areas giving way to bilberry in the east. Patches of wet heath or bogland, with sphagnum and cotton grass, break up the landscape. The hills were earmarked by the War Office in 1946 as the site for a permanent military training area, involving the expulsion from their homes of over two hundred farmers, however a campaign launched in opposition proved vigorous enough for the Government to abandon it's plans in 1948. There are smaller areas of low lying heath at Strumble Head and St David's Head. Roadside verges, and traditional hedgebanks, whether of stone and/or turf, are ablaze with the colours of wild flowers in spring and early summer. The semi-natural specialised grassland of farms have less to offer in terms of wildlife, though many have areas of waste ground, or a pond. In the south the limestone cliffs and plateau, with it's short springy turf and superb maritime flora, is one of the most impressive limestone areas in Britain.

Geologically Pembrokeshire is of spectacular interest. Not only does it offer magnificently exposed rock formations around it's coast, but the series of rocks on display range in an unbroken series from the very oldest Pre-Cambrian, from 3,000 million years ago, to the Carboniferous coal measures of 300 million years ago. The Pre-Cambrian rocks, formed before the appearance of any obvious fossilized life, occur in a small area extending from Whitesands Bay to Porth Llysgi. Later Lower Palaeozoic rocks, the Cambrian, Ordovician and Silurian systems which begin 570 million years ago, occur, like the Pre-Cambrian, in the north of the county. These igneous and sedimentary rocks were faulted and folded at the end of the Silurian period, some 400 million years ago, during the great Caledonian earth movements. As a result a WSW – ENE grain was imposed across the north of the county; one further result being the formation of St David's peninsula.

By contrast the rocks in south Pembrokeshire are mainly Upper Palaeozoic. Devonian Old Red Sandstone covers most of the north side of Milford Haven, Dale and Angle peninsulas, and part of Caldey Island, while a superb limestone section runs from Linney Head to Stackpole Head, with further sections at Lydstep and Giltar Point at Penally. A significant coal measure runs across the county from Saundersfoot to St Brides Bay. After the depositions of the coal measures the land was again subject to massive earth movements, this time the Armorican orogeny of 290 million years ago. However now a WNW – ESE grain was imposed across the south of the county.

The present flatness of the land is due to constant wave erosion at a time when the sea covered the landscape, probably during the late Tertiary period some 17,000 million years ago. Only the more resistant igneous outcrops, like Carn Llidi and Garn Fawr, remained as islands above the sea. Recent evidence suggests that Britain's status as an island began some time between 450,000 and 200,000 years ago when the natural land dam between the Strait of Dover and France was destroyed in a megaflood, with a wall of water forced through it with at least ten times the force of the Boxing Day tsunami of 2004. Earliest human presence in Britain has been dated back to 840,000, possibly 950,000 years ago, but between 180,000 and 60,000 years ago all evidence of human presence dies out. Even during glaciation and low sea levels the newly formed Channel river seems to have acted as a barrier to further human occupation until some 60,000 years ago when sea levels fell to a low enough level for crossing. Whilst Britain was periodically cut off from France by the new Channel river until 6,100 BC Britain had retained a land link with the Netherlands, Germany and Denmark, an area known as Doggerland, and which would during the Mesolithic era, when free of ice, have provided a rich hunting ground. However a submarine landslide off Norway triggered another megatsunami, and Doggerland was submerged to leave Britain finally an island, and it's Mesolithic population cut off from mainland Europe.

On at least two occasions Pembrokeshire lay under the Irish Sea glacier; the first occasion, some 120,000 years ago, covered the entire county, while the second, 20 to 17,000 years ago, affected only the north. Before the advent of this last ice sheet drove him south Palaeolithic man, Old Stone Age man, had made his appearance, living in caves on Caldey Island and at Hoyle's Mouth near Penally. 15,000 years ago the climate became gradually warmer, the land was re-colonised, and with the melting of the ice under the glacier deep and narrow gorges, originally formed with the initial retreat of the glacier, were further deepened as the meltwater scythed it's way to the sea. Cwm Gwaun is the most impressive example of a meltwater channel in Britain. With the final melting of the ice, and the rise in sea levels some 10,000 years ago, the existing river valleys of Milford Haven and Solva were drowned by the incoming tides, assuming their present shape, and the forests were gradually submerged to remain exposed at coastal beaches, as at Whitesands Bay and Amroth, at low tides.

Mesolithic culture began to develop in the county some 10,500 years ago, with Mesolithic man continuing to live, much as his ancestor Palaeolithic man had done, by hunting and fishing, with perhaps a little primitive farming, and some movement to open settlement in flimsy shelters. However it was a change in the use of stone tools that marked one cultural difference – there have been finds of his flint tools at Nab Head near St Brides Haven, Swanlake Bay near Manorbier, and on Caldey Island. Much of the marshy wooded lowlands where he hunted gradually fell under the encroaching sea – perhaps the tales of great floods, lost cities, and the fine towns of Cantref Gwaelod (the Netherlands of Cardigan Bay) are folk memories of these drowned lands.

This Mesolithic hunter-gatherer society gradually gave way some 6,000 years ago to the Neolithic era. With the Neolithic age came a new relationship with the land; the given environment was modified to include domesticated wheat and barley, sheep, cattle and goats. This meant the clearance of the woodland and fixed settlement, a settled home in the natural landscape of the Mesolithic era. It has long been heralded that this

Neolithic farming revolution was introduced into Wales, as Britain, by incomers, with the Mesolithic inhabitants forced into the margins, but perhaps it was a more a mixture of the migration of ideas and settlers that forged the new society. Of their day to day settlements, made of wood (only in the Orkneys at the tip of Scotland did the climate require stone) little survives – there is a single trace at Clegyr Boia, near St David's. However the landscape they inhabited is marked by ritual reminders of their presence, the great stone burial chambers. Perhaps with kinship with the land came the need to express that kinship through ritual possession of the landscape through reminders of their ancestors – longevity of kin given expression in stone and earth, the symbol of territory and ownership of landscape. There are fine examples of their burial chambers at Pentre Ifan near Nevern, one of the finest in Britain, with others, plentiful along the north coast and on the Preseli hills, rarer in the south.

It has been argued that the late Neolithic/early Bronze Age eras heralded the development of a new ideology and society associated with the rising and setting sun and moon. There was a new emphasis on the way of the heavens. Along with the decline in monumental burial chambers – they were replaced by single round burial chambers built on higher and more visible ground than their predecessors, as at Foel Drygarn in the Preseli hills, went the building of stone circles, henges and stone alignments; these processional alignments could be interpreted as processional journeys from death to the afterlife. There is a fine stone circle at Gors Fawr, near Mynachlog Ddu in the Preseli hills. There seems to have been a desertion of settlements and a re-establishment of cleared woodland, though the agricultural system appears to have remained stable. It is believed that the arrival of the Bronze Age (2,200 to 700 BC) was heralded by the immigration of the Beaker people from Europe (so called because of their characteristic decorated pottery drinking vessels), carrying knowledge of copper and bronze, and it's use in weaponry and jewellery, but again as with the Neolithic, it may have been as much a movement of ideas and trade.

The late Bronze Age witnessed a world wide deterioration in climate and widespread movements of population in Europe. There was freezing weather and perpetual rain, along with famine and crop failures; at one time the cause was attributed to a volcanic explosion in Iceland, now it is thought a comet passing near the earth's atmosphere in 1159 BC smothered the earth in a dust cloud, blotting out the sun for eighteen summers. Upland areas were abandoned, and for the first time pressure on farmland resulted in the building of defensive settlements. Strategic sites favoured were coastal headlands and hilltops; this pattern continued with the gradual development of iron working, and as the Iron Age progresses society takes on a more aggressive face – the larger forts perhaps exercising some control over the smaller defended settlements with regional grouping forming the basis of future tribal areas. The Deer Park fort by Marloes makes full use of it's coastal setting and natural defensive position, likewise the inland forts of Foel Drygarn (superimposed on the Bronze Age burial site) and Carn Ingli by Newport. Castell Henllys, near Nevern, is a superb re-creation of an Iron Age settlement, and well worth a visit. One long standing theory has it that it was at the beginning of the Iron Age that the Celts arrived in numbers in Britain, speaking the ancestors of the modern Celtic languages, however there is no evidence to suggest any major influx of people. The so called 'Celtic' languages may date back to the late Neolithic/early Bronze Age, if not earlier; how and when they arrived in Britain is not known. Society as it developed would have come under the influence of the 'Celtic' mores of Iron Age Europe – the only real Celts at the time were the continental Gauls, though Classical commentators had begun to refer to these Iron Age European peoples as Celts from 500 BC onwards.

The Roman period begins with Julius Caesar's landing on the Kent coastline in 55 BC, however Romanisation of the country proper begins with the invasion of Claudius in AD 43 – by AD 78 the conquest of Wales was complete. Existing tribal groupings in southern Wales were the Silures of the south-east, with, to the west, the Demetae. The conquest of the Demetae seems to have been quick and efficient, and whilst there is little evidence of Roman settlement west of the fort at Carmarthen recent finds of a substantial villa near Wolfscastle, and traces of a road leading from Carmarthen towards Haverfordwest suggest Roman influence may be greater than once thought. With the collapse of Roman rule in the early 5th century the pattern of small scale farming continued, much as it had done during the Iron Age, with services and obligations owed by smaller farmers and bondsmen to the 'nobles'. However the removal of a central authority left the land open to raids, first by the Irish – an Irish dynasty was most probably in power in west Wales by the end of the 5th century – and later by the Vikings, who in addition to destroying many settlements, including St David's monastic settlement on several occasions, gave their own names to many of the more prominent landmarks; Grassholm, Skokholm and Solva all have Norse connections.

The 5th and 6th centuries was the Age of the Saints, when peregrini, travelling monks from Europe and Ireland, helped consolidate the hold of Christianity in Wales and lay the foundations of the Celtic church. Central to the local community was the *llan*, so common a feature of Welsh place names, and being an enclosure, often circular (and often making use of an already circular site) for burial. Manorbier's churchyard is of this type. Other early Christian evidence derives from the many Christian stones, inscribed with the names of the aristocracy, and marking the site of their graves. Some of the earliest are in Latin and/or ogham – ogham an Irish script of cut notches along the edge of the stone to indicate spelling, an indication of early Irish presence in the area. There is a fine example in Cilgerran's churchyard. Ogham had ceased by 600, later stones being in Latin. More elaborate stones, decorated with linework and fine crosses, may have marked church property. There are two decorated 10th to 11th century crosses in Penally church, near Tenby, which may have been carved for a monastic settlement in the vicinity.

One pioneer of the new church was St David, who established his monastic settlement in the St David's area – his original monastery may have been at Whitesands Bay, rather than on the site of the present cathedral. The community's way of life was based on worship and hard manual labour. No oxen were used in ploughing, the yoke was put to their own shoulders, and once labour was completed time was given to contemplation. Diet was vegetarian, based on bread and herbs, and, probably, water, though what was their main type of drink is uncertain. With the new monasticism came a new mysticism and asceticism. Ascetics chose solitary places to reside, often living in *clochan* – beehive shaped buildings made of local stone. There is at Pwll Deri near Strumble Head, in Tal y Gaer farmyard, a building which may well have been a clochan of this

type. Pembrokeshire's islands, beaches and coves offered further opportunities for the solitary; St Govan's near Bosherston, with it's chapel in a cleft of rock, is one of the best known – the ocean for these ascetics often

St Govan's chapel

replaced the desert of the Egyptian fathers. The Age of the Saints was also the heroic age of Britain, the age of Arthur, defender of civilisation after the Roman collapse to barbarism. The 11th and 12th century Welsh tales of the Mabinogion relate some of the earliest tales of Arthur in literature; Culhwch and Olwen telling of Arthur and his knights' hunt of a magical boar across St David's peninsula, the Nyfer valley and the Preseli hills.

The years 400 to 600 were crucial to the formation of Wales as a country, as it was to the Scottish and English nations, and it is the fortunes of the early kingdoms and their rulers that give the period the political flavour of the age. By the mid 10th century it was possible, if only temporarily, for Hywel Dda (*Hywel 'the Good'*) to have added the kingdom of Deheubarth (Cardiganshire, Pembrokeshire, Carmarthenshire and Gower) to the northern and eastern kingdoms of Gwynedd and Powys, and to have consolidated the Law of Wales, quite possibly at a meeting held at Whitland in west Carmarthenshire. However by the late 11th century a new and feared power was in the land.

The Norman conquest of 1066 was to change the face of Wales, as it had done England's. The occupation of England had already traumatised existing society, and the conduct of the campaign had led to comment on the ensuing *sacrifice of human life* by Pope Gregory VII in 1080, ally to William I; in the expeditions of 1069-70 in the north of England the surviving population had been left to starvation and cannibalism. Initially Rhys ap Tewdwr managed to retain his rule over Deheubarth, though acknowledging overlordship to William who crossed his lands in 1081 on a 'pilgrimage' to St David's – no doubt he also visited Whitesands Bay, the normal embarkation point for Ireland, and a possible embarkation point for any invasion of Ireland. However after Rhys' death a series of lordships were established in this south-western corner of the Marches of Wales. Moving from his base on the Severn, Roger, Earl of Shrewsbury, crossed into Pembrokeshire by way of Cardiganshire, his son establishing the Lordship of Pembroke. Castles were built at Roch in the west, and Wiston, Llawhaden, Narberth and Amroth on Carmarthen Bay – with isolated Norman settlements in the north at Newport and Cilgerran. For a time an almost definable frontier stretched across the centre of the county – a convenient dividing line later termed the Landsker (poss. Norse for frontier) by later historians. Early castles were earth and timber, either ringwork, or motte and bailey, and sited not only on strategic high points, but also close to the rivers and sea-lanes. With consolidation of power and the continuing need for defence stone was used – Pembroke one of the finest and most impregnable, and consequently one of the few never to be occupied by the Welsh, who continued to oppose Norman settlement by force of arms.

Pembroke castle

South Pembrokeshire formed part of the Marches of Wales, a region where taxes and law were the prerogatives of the lords in the castle. The new colony was organised on the English pattern, the first such in Wales, and had, by at least 1138, independent 'palatine' status. This is the basis of Pembrokeshire's claim to be the premier county of Wales. Prior to the Norman arrival villages had been the largest settlements; with colonisation came the development of Anglo-Norman towns, with Pembroke the first county town west of the Severn. The creation of *Little England beyond Wales* was underway. The local population was absorbed into the growing Norman colony, supplemented by English, Irish and Flemish settlers. To the north the Welsh maintained their way of life, and their own language; in the castles the new lords planned the consolidation of their power through the language of French. Until the Edwardian conquest of Wales in 1282 Wales outside the Marches – *pura Wallia* (pure or non Norman Wales) – was allowed to retain it's separate identity.

Pre-eminent amongst the Welsh princes of the 12th century was the Lord Rhys, Rhys ap Gruffydd. He ruled from the Welsh stronghold of Deheubarth at Dinefwr castle in Carmarthenshire, which may be his work. It was a time of stability for Welsh culture; he hosted the first eisteddfod at Cardigan castle in 1176, with competitors arriving from abroad as well as other parts of Wales. He founded an abbey at Talley in Carmarthenshire, and rebuilt Cardigan castle in stone. After his death Llywelyn the Great held sway; however with his death in 1282, and the end of the Welsh drive for independence, (until the Owain Glyndŵr uprising in the early 15th century), the Welsh princes ruled under a watchful English eye. To serve the lords in the castle traders and craftsmen settled close by, and in time these communities were granted trade rights and privileges, and later charters confirming borough status. This pattern of urban growth, imitated by the Welsh princes, formed the basis of the urban structure of Wales until the Industrial Revolution.

Norman society was nothing if not rigid; at the head of it's structure was God, with the King and villein all bound to those above by duty. The expression of that social order was in land, the great estates of the Norman lords, and the obligations of their feudal tenants. The most fertile land was given to their followers, the Welsh were forced to the uplands where they were allowed to keep their customs and law, whilst in the new urban areas settlement was restricted, at least initially, to the non Welsh. Of the medieval strip field system there are survivals at Angle. Inevitably the Normans found the Celtic church too independent and outdated, and it was quickly remodelled along Continental lines. St David's became one of four Welsh dioceses, with outlying churches organised into a parish system; new churches with defensive towers being built on the old *llannau*, and the dedications to Celtic saints usually being removed and rededicated to Roman ones. Celtic monasticism was also tied to Europe and European orders – a new Cistercian monastery was established at Whitland in 1140. At no time was St David's ever garrisoned, though an Episcopal system was imposed, and in 1181 work began on a new cathedral.

It may be possible that the asceticism that was contemporary with St David and his followers continued through the centuries; certainly there is evidence for ascetic practice during the 11th and early 12th centuries. The Age of the Saints provided plenty of legends and holy sites, some newly founded, for an aspiring ascetic, and for the growing number of pilgrims to St David's hospitals were built by Norman bishops at Llawhaden and Whitewell at St David's, with sister's houses at Minwear on the eastern Cledddau, and possibly at Angle. Abbeys, priories and chapels were built, as at St Dogmael's, Haverfordwest and St Non's. The Knights Hospitallers of St John of Jerusalem had their Welsh headquarters at Slebech, on the opposite side of the river to Minwear, where they administered to the sick and recruited for the Crusades. Yet for all their piety there was a dark side to the Norman vision. The Celtic vision had been one of nature mysticism and humanity, the Normans introduced savage visions of heaven and hell.

By the time of the accession to the English throne in 1485 of Henry VII, born in Pembroke castle, society in the Marches and in Wales as a whole had become more peaceful and orderly. Castles could be modified to become comfortable manor houses, as at Carew, and the Welsh gentry who had leant their support to Henry Tudor as he had taken to the field against Richard III at Bosworth were suitably

Carew castle

rewarded. There was greater opportunity for social mobility in society as a whole, and the growth of urban life, the most marked effect of the Norman conquest, continued. The Acts of Union of 1536-43 marked the political merger of Wales with England. The power of the Norman Lords and their independence was ended and Pembrokeshire was made a county, with, for the first time, much the same boundaries as now, and the dissolution of the monasteries ended the power of the abbeys. Pilgrimages were now seen as idolatrous. A new faith was in the land, and all power was under the control of the king, Henry VIII.

In the centuries that followed life came to be dominated by the demands of agriculture and trade, and the years from the Acts of Union to 1770 have been characterised as the age of the gentry, of the rise of the yeoman farmer. It was they who received the bulk of economic surplus and who exercised control over the destiny of their fellow men. The Acts of Union had abolished the privileges of the Marches of Wales tying the fortunes of their lords to those of Henry VIII's state. The dissolution of the monasteries in 1540 similarly asserted the authority of the Tudor state. Following the break with Rome the Church of England was established, but it is open to debate how wholeheartedly the new church was adopted. In the towns those that had access to the sea grew into flourishing ports, and every small creek and cove seemed to have it's own sloop, often locally built. Out went wool, cattle and grain, and in came general merchandise, wine and spices, not to mention the often highly profitable smuggled cargo. The

Civil War of the mid 17th century raised tensions and politics between neighbours – the Welsh mainly favoured the king, while the south were, usually, for Parliament – but if politics were uncertain and allegiances inconstant the underlying economy remained stable. Allegiance was finally settled at the Battle of Colby Moor, near Wiston on the A40, on 1 August 1645, when a Royalist army was defeated by Parliamentary forces at the cost of 150 Royalists killed, with over 700 taken prisoner. It was during the Civil War that the castles saw their last moments of glory; however any which had served the Royalist cause were quickly rendered defenceless by Cromwell after victory. Many were left to fade into obscurity, to find uses in later centuries as Romantic ruins.

The 19th century had as profound an effect on Pembrokeshire as had the arrival of the Normans. The coming of the railways in mid and late century heralded new communication and commercial advantages. Visitors began to arrive in increasing numbers at resort towns such as Tenby and Manorbier, already growing in importance during the late 18th century. Three new towns were established on the shores around Milford Haven. Neyland, previously a small fishing village, was planned by Brunel as the terminus of his South Wales railway, and as the terminus of Irish and transatlantic steamships – however there was little Atlantic shipping and the Irish service was to transfer to Fishguard in 1906. Milford Haven was laid out as a private initiative in 1793; among the earliest settlers a group of Quaker whalers from Nantucket. By 1900 to 1914 the town had risen to become one of the busiest fishing ports in the country. Across the water Pembroke Dock grew with the Admiralty dockyard established there in 1814 – for much of the century it was the world's most advanced shipyard, with revolutionary warships and five royal yachts to it's credit.

There were many local industrial concerns. Coal mining had always been of importance, production reaching it's peak during the late 18th and early 19th centuries at sites on St Brides Bay, at the confluence of the eastern and western Cleddau, and in the Saundersfoot and Kilgetty area. To exploit the latter's many pits the Saundersfoot Railway and Harbour Company was formed in 1829, and nearby, in Pleasant Valley, the Stepaside Ironworks flourished from 1849 to 1877. Whole villages were given over to quarrying, as at Cilgerran, and at Porthgain and Abereiddi where slates and bricks were also produced. Many of these concerns were comparatively shortlived, and had ceased operating by early or mid 20th century; Hook, on the western Cleddau, was the last colliery, closing in 1949, Porthgain's industrial age ended in 1931, and the Saundersfoot Railway and Harbour Company rail lines were raised by the 1940s. There were changes in agriculture too, cheap fertilizers raised yields and meant the end of the centuries old lime burning industry; cheap imported grain milled in larger town mills meant the end of local flour and feed producing mills, and cheap metals spelt the end of the local smithy. The revolution in land transport meant the end of the coastal trade, and local shipbuilding. The coming of the railways spelt the end also for the centuries old trade of the drovers, who had herded cattle, sheep, pigs and geese over the hills and byways of Pembrokeshire from local farms to the fattening fields and markets of England. However change did not come without problems. The imposition of what were seen as harsh rents and rates, taxes and tolls, demanded by the squierarchy and magistrates led to the smashing of turnpike gates in 1839 and the early 1840s. Dressed in women's clothes, and led by Rebecca, the Rebecca Rioters nightly smashed gates and burnt down the toll houses all across west Wales. As it said in Genesis 24 verse 60 *And they blessed Rebecca, and said unto her, Thou art our sister, be thou the mother of thousands of millions, and let thy seed possess the gate of those which hate them.* Following Government legislation revoking many of the grievances matters began to improve.

Politically the introduction of county councils in the late 1880s, with elected officials, replaced the centuries rule by the squierarchy, the local landowners who on a voluntary basis had occupied the leading positions in the county. The 19th century was also the hey-day of non conformism, active since the 17th century. Chapels, built out of subscriptions raised by local congregations, began to appear in ever increasing numbers in the towns and villages, particularly in the Welsh speaking areas. Indeed as public buildings the chapels are more truly the Welsh vernacular architecture than the great Norman castles. It was also the age of the restoration of the existing Norman and Celtic churches. Since the Reformation there had been little new church building, and existing churches had been either barely maintained or allowed to decay. Old ones were renovated, and new ones, with inventive variations on existing styles, were built, as at Capel Colman in the north east of the county near Boncath.

By the mid 20th century modernisation had transformed the county. 1960 saw the first oil port, Esso, established. Though Esso closed in 1983 Milford Haven's claim to be a leading energy port has been boosted by the arrival of two new Liquid Natural Gas (LNG) import and storage facilities in the shape of South Hook LNG, and the smaller Dragon LNG, which together with the new gas fired power station at Pembroke and the Valero and Murco oil refineries form a modern energy portfolio. The energy industry, agriculture and tourism, the public services and the small business sector are now the backbones of the local economy. Pembrokeshire was designated Britain's first coastal National Park in 1952, and the long distance Coast Path was opened in 1970. The Coast Path will form part of the planned All Wales Coast Path. Scheduled to be open by 2012 it will, together with Offa's Dyke Path, make for a testing circular walk around all of Wales. Pembrokeshire returned as a county in it's own right in April 1996, having been from 1974 part of the larger county of Dyfed – the National Park was similarly made a separate authority.

history of the pub
It is thought the first inns date back to Roman times, when inns and the smaller *tavernae*, or taverns, were established alongside the newly built roads for officials

and other travellers. Alcohol served was largely wine, imported from the empire, though ale brewed from cereals may also have been served; almost certainly the secrets of brewing were known in Britain by the Neolithic period. The later Saxons continued the tradition of the tavern, each village having houses where court could be held, and ale drunk. By the time the Normans had established power the creation of towns in the shadow of the castles included the establishment of permanent ale houses sited often close by the market square and church. They reintroduced wine, and popularised the drinking of cider, however ale remained the drink of choice. In Pembrokeshire, with the growth of St David's as a shrine, inns were opened to provide for pilgrims and travellers – Pope Calixtus II is credited with equating two pilgrimages to St David's with one to Rome; it was also said that three was the equal of one to Jerusalem.

There was a strong link between the monasteries and the brewing industry, the monasteries creating guest houses and hospices, often offering free bread and ale. Guests however were usually restricted to the upper classes and pilgrims, the middle and lower classes staying in inns. Though definitions were to later become blurred an inn provided rooms, the tavern food and drink, while the humble ale house served only ale. Whilst monks were well known as brewers, funds for the monastery raised by sale, it was traditionally, as with the baking of bread, women's work, excess being sold on. Regulation of the trade came early on, with the Magna Carta including a decree to standardise the measure for corn, wine and ale – the latter the origins of the measure of a pint.

One major revolution in drinking habits was the 15th century introduction of hops from Europe, where they had been in use from the 8th century. The result was the introduction of a new drink – beer. Ale remained the first choice for a long time since it was untainted by the preservative hop flower – giving a sharper flavour, whilst ale was stronger and sweeter. Prior to introduction of the hop ale had been flavoured with herbs like rosemary. However beer had better keeping properties, and by the mid 16th century Dutch and Flemish immigrants had well established hop gardens in Kent and Sussex. With the dissolution of the monasteries by Henry VIII from 1538 onwards the pattern of accommodation inevitably changed, wealthy travellers and pilgrims now seeking the shelter of the more substantial town inns that began to develop, with reasonable rooms, food and stabling on offer.

By the 18th century public houses were being purpose built, offering several rooms for different classes of drinkers, but without however offering accommodation. Many ale houses, often one room affairs, upgraded, others continuing their trade serving the lower classes. The improvements in the road network and of the horse drawn coach transformed many of the existing inns into coaching inns, with the better town inns adding function rooms to their business portfolio. The development of seaside resorts like Tenby encouraged similar expansion. Further developments saw the beginnings of the tied house, the brewer making deliveries to particular pubs in his area, and the brewer's dray – the low heavy horse cart used for haulage – became a familiar sight in the towns.

Drinking habits had seen a large increase in brandy and gin consumption since the late 17th century onwards, and there had been a number of acts introduced to curb the habit and turn the taste back to beer, seen as more wholesome, water being boiled as part of the brewing process. Part of the problem had been the exemption of spirits from duty, whilst it remained payable on beer. The introduction of the 1830 Beer Act sought to curb spirit consumption and promote agriculture and beer by abolishing the beer duty and introducing the beer shop, or beer house. For the small sum of two guineas any householder could obtain a beer licence to sell beer and cider only, the public houses retaining the right to sell also spirits and wine. The result was thousands of new beer houses, with many tradesmen adding the sale of beer as a sideline. However the beer shops were often poorly run, leading to outbreaks of drunken behaviour. They soon became known as Tom and Jerry shops, so named after two Regency bucks from Tom Egan's 1821 comic serial *Life In London*, featuring the often disreputable adventures of Corinthian Tom and his country cousin Jerry Hawthorne – the original Tom and Jerry.

Alongside the rise in Tom and Jerry shops went the rise in the Temperance movement. Organised in 1828 the movement had favoured the development of the beer shop, some members quite happy to recommend beer and wine when drunk in moderation. However moves were afoot to curb Sunday opening hours, and by mid century ways were sought to curb the numbers of beer houses altogether. The 1869 Wine and Beer House Act gave control of all licensed premises to the magistrate; with the result that many smaller premises closed, and with little possibility of new ones opening the larger brewers began to extend their control – the introduction of refrigeration in the 1880s further helped industrialisation. 1881 saw the introduction of the Welsh Sunday Closing Act. Each movement of religious revival in Wales was accompanied by temperance promotion, many local landowners in Pembrokeshire, notably at Stackpole and Lawrenny, lending their support by outlawing pubs on their estates. By 1914 and the Defence of the Realm Act even tighter laws were introduced, it became illegal to buy anyone a drink, even your mate, the practice of treating seen as encouraging excessive drinking. A culture of excessive drinking among servicemen and munitions workers was a great fear, drink being identified as being as much the enemy as Germany in certain political quarters.

By the 1930s attitudes to the pub, to drinking, and to temperance were changing. Pubs were coming to be seen as social centres, rather than as a centre for drunkenness, and calls for a return to the restrictions of the Great War were rejected. The post 1945 growth of tourism favoured the development of the pub, and 1961 saw the introduction of the Licensing Act giving the choice to counties to reject Sunday closing. Pembrokeshire went wet in 1968. The 1960s and 1970s witnessed a trend towards extension of existing pubs in tourist areas, with some new ones opening as with the Lawrenny Arms, and with refurbishment of others, though with hindsight the 1970s idea of style was not always of the best. Others resisted and retain their original character, notably the Dyffryn Arms in Cwm Gwaun. One other major change of recent years has been the growth in favour of keg beers, the 1960s consolidation of the brewing industry led to the closure of many small brewers, and the move to develop a stable beer with a longer shelf life. Unlike real ale, which undergoes a secondary fermentation normally in the pub cellar, keg beer has been pasteurised, thus killing off the beer bacteria that causes fermentation by heating – CO_2 being then added. One response to this was the formation of the Campaign for Real Ale, CAMRA, in 1971. The 21st century has seen a keen interest in local beer in Wales, with over forty micro-breweries established in all parts of the country. Local ales in north Pembrokeshire can be found at the Cwm Gwaun Brewery, which is located on a farm in the valley and is open to the public, and at the Nag's Head, Abercych.

Another recent change was the implementation of the Licensing Act of 2003, which transferred the responsibility for licensing from the magistrate to local councils, which are now termed the Licensing Authority. Included in the act was the potential for 24 hour opening, seven days a week. Further changes in April 2007 saw a ban on smoking in the work place in Wales, including the pub.

history of inn signs

Trade signs can be traced back to the Ancient Egyptians, with their use proliferating during Roman times. Normally Roman signs would be a relief carving in terracotta or stone, with a common symbol to indicate the trade, for example a dairy  would be represented by a goat. With the Roman occupation of Britain the common Roman practice of hanging vine leaves outside a tavern to indicate it's purpose had to be replaced by the hanging of an evergreen bush – Britain's inclement weather did not favour the vine. If only ale was sold then the ale stake or the long pole used to stir the ale was displayed, if both wine and ale were on sale then both bush and pole would be put out. With the abandonment of Britain by Rome the use of some form of signage persisted, with early tavern signs directed at the largely illiterate population based on religion, with the Cross, the Cross Keys, the Star and the Sun common images. By the 12th century it had become normal practice for inns to be individually named. However the symbol displayed soon became evidence of power, with the choice of image often being mandatory. In 1393 Richard II required his own personal emblem of the White Hart to be displayed to identify London inns to his official ale taster; in 1603, with James VI of Scotland becoming James I of England, all important buildings, including taverns, were required to display the Red Lion of Scotland. Development of inn signs mirrored the changes in society and trade as a whole, Railway taverns, Smugglers Haunts and Jolly Sailors being added to the signs of religion, nobility and royalty, and indication of place. The Three Horseshoes for example takes it's sign from that of the Worshipful Company of Farriers, usually thereby indicating the local landlord was also the blacksmith. In Wales the Red Dragon has became a favoured alternative to the Red Lion.

place-names

The study of place-names is a fascinating branch of local history in it's own right, indicating geographical features which may have vanished, patterns of former land ownership, forgotten buildings or former trades. However the current place name may be far removed from the original name, particularly where there is an anglicised form of an old Welsh name, for example Pembroke is derived from *Pen Fro*, the Welsh for Land's End. Welsh place names are particularly expressive of geography, and can be highly poetic, for example Pwll Deri, pool of the oak trees. Some of the more common names are listed below:

Aber – river mouth, estuary
Afon – river
Ar – on, over
Bach/Fach – little
Ban/Fan(au) – peak, crest, beacon

Banc – bank
Barcud – kite
Bedd – grave
Bedw – birch
Blaen – top
Bre – hill
Bryn – hill

Bwlch – pass
Caer(au) – fort(s)
Canol – middle, centre
Cantref – hundred
    (ancient land area)
Capel – chapel
Carn/Garn – cairn
Carreg, pl cerrig – rock,
    stone
Castell – castle
Cefn – ridge
Cil – nook, source of
    stream
Clawdd – ditch
Cleddau – sword
Clyn/Clun – meadow
Coch – red
Coed – wood
Coetref/Goetre –woodland,
    homestead
Cors/Gors – bog, marsh
Craig – rock, cliff
Crib – ridge
Croes – cross
Cromlech(au) – burial
    mound(s)
Cwm – valley
Cwrw – beer
Cyhoeddus – public
Dan – under
Darren – rocky hillside

Dau – two
Deri – oak tree
Dinas – hill fort
Dôl – meadow
Du/Ddu – black
Dŵr – water
Efail – smithy
Eglwys – church
Esgair – ridge
Ffordd – road
Ffrwd – stream, torrent
Ffynnon – fountain, well,
    spring
Gallt/Allt – hill, cliff, wood
Gelli – grove
Glan – river bank
Glas – blue, green
Gwaun – moor, meadow
Gwyn/Gwen – white
Gwynt – wind
Hafod – summer dwelling
Hen – old
Hendre – winter dwelling
Heol – road
Isaf – lower
Lan – ascent
Llaethdy – dairy
Llan, pl llannau – church,
    village
Llech – flat stone
Llyn – lake

Llwybr – path, track
Llwyd/lwyd – brown, grey; pale; hoary
Llwyn – grove, bush
Llydan – broad, wide
Maen – rock, stone
Maes – field
Marchog – horseman, rider, knight
Mawr/Fawr – great, big
Meddyg – doctor, physician
Melin – mill
Melyn – yellow
Moel/Foel – bare topped hill
Mwyn – ore, mineral
Mynydd – mountain
Nant – brook, stream
Newydd – new
Nos – night
Ogof – cave
Pant – hollow, valley
Parc – field, park

Pen – head, top
Penlan – top of hill
Pentre – village
Plas – hall
Pont – bridge
Porth – harbour
Picws – peak
Pwll – pool
Rhiw – hill
Rhos – moorland
Rhyd – ford
Sir – county, shire
Tafarn – inn
Tir – land, ground, territory
Traeth – beach
Tref – town, hamlet
Tri/tair – three
Tŷ – house
Uchaf – upper
Y/Yr – the
Yn – in
Ynys – island
Ysgol – school

A few notes on pronunciation:

c – k (hard)
ch – as in lo*ch*
dd – th as in th*at*
f – v

ff – f
g – g (hard)
ll – pronounce l, keep tongue in position at roof of mouth, and hiss!
th – th as in *th*ink

There are 7 vowels, a, e, i, o, u, w and y. Pronunciation may be long or short.

w may be as in pool, or pull eg *cwm* (coom) – valley
y may be as in fun, or pin eg *y, yr* (u, ur) – the, *dyffryn* (dufrin) – valley

Many Welsh words change their pronunciation and spelling under certain circumstances, for example the initial consonant of many words may soften: b to f, c to g, m to f, p to b etc. Common examples of mutations are bach (little) to fach, mawr (big) to fawr, porth (harbour) to borth. Such mutations can make tracing words through a dictionary a little problematic.

One important Welsh word to know in a book on pub walks is *cwrw* (curoo) – beer.

tourist information centres

Cardigan – Theatr Mwldan, Bath House Road
01239 613230
Goodwick (Fishguard Harbour) – Ocean Lab, ˎ
The Parrog   01348 872037

Fishguard – The Town Hall, Market Square

01437 776636

Haverfordwest – 19 Old Bridge   01437 763110
Milford Haven – Suite 19, Cedar Court   01437 771818
Newport National Park – 2 Banc Cottages,
Long Street   01239 820912
Pembroke – Commons Road   01437 776499
St David's National Park – Oriel y Parc,
Landscape Gallery, The Grove   01437 720392

Saundersfoot – The Barbecue, The Harbour

01834 813672

Tenby – Unit 2, Upper Park Road   01834 842402
Tenby National Park – Ruabon House,
South Parade   01834 845040

the country code

Enjoy the countryside and respect it's life and work.
Guard against all risk of fire.
Fasten all gates.
Keep your dogs under close control.
Keep to public paths across farmland.
Use gates and stiles to cross fences, hedges and walls.
Leave livestock, crops and machinery alone.
Take your litter home.
Help to keep all water clean.
Protect wildlife, plants and trees.
Take special care on county roads.
Make no unnecessary noise.

hazards and problems
take notice, take care

The author and the publishers stresses that walkers should be aware of the dangers that may occur on all walks.

Check local weather forecast before walking; do not walk up into mist or low clouds.

Use local OS maps side by side with walking guides.

Wear walking boots and appropriate clothing.

Do not take any unnecessary risks – conditions can change suddenly and can vary from season to season.

Take special care when accompanied by children or dogs.

When walking on roads, ensure that you are conspicuous to traffic from either direction.

Please note that the terms 'easier', 'easy' are only used in this book in comparison to the most dangerous and challenging routes when you are out walking.

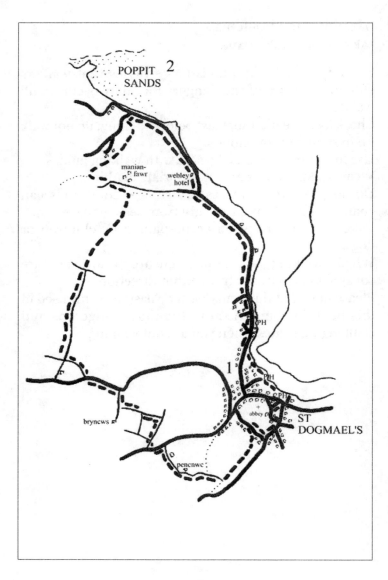

POPPIT
SANDS

2

manian-
fawr

webley
hotel

PH

1

PH

PH

bryncws

abbey

ST
DOGMAEL'S

pencnwc

1. st ðoGmael's anð poppit sanðs

6.25 miles/10 kilometres

OS Maps: 1:25 000 North Pembrokeshire Outdoor Leisure 35.

Start: The Moorings, close by the Ferry Inn St Dogmael's.

Access: St Dogmael's is on the B4546 road leading to Poppit Sands from the main Cardigan road. Bus 405 the Poppit Rocket and bus 407 stop at St Dogmael's en route from Cardigan to Poppit Sands. The bus stop for the start (and end) of the walk is the Moorings.

Parking: Parking just past the Ferry Inn (on the road leading out to Poppit Sands from the centre of town), at the side of the road by the landing stage opposite the residential street of the Moorings. Limited parking for patrons at the inn itself. There is a car park in the village itself, well signposted. Car park also at Poppit Sands.

Grade: Moderate.

The Ferry Inn, Poppit Road, St Dogmael's, Cardigan (01239 615172)

Traceable back to the 1840s this popular river pub was much enlarged in 1972 with the building of a restaurant at the back of the pub. Later additions were the decked terraces to back and side, giving superb views over the river Teifi and adjacent countryside. Lots of local memorabilia inside. Pub/restaurant. Dogs welcome outside on the terrace.

Teifi Netpool Inn, St Dogmael's, Cardigan (01239 612680)

The inn takes it's name from one of the prized salmon pools on the river Teifi. Close to the inn the Teifi netpool was matched by the Cardigan netpool on the other side of the river. Seine fishing involved the rowing out of a net across the river, to be then hauled in when it's full extent was reached. To ensure fairness in who fished which pool lots were drawn each day at the inn, a bag of numbered pebbles hung in the porch for this purpose. At the end of the day fish caught were weighed and sold at the inn. The nets used were hung on frames, known as standards, still sited on the area in front of the inn, both to dry and for repairs; they were dipped in tannin for preservation. Just below the inn, alongside the river, was the *Pinog*, where the salmon boats were beached and where boats were built. The inn has many photographs of St Dogmael's fishing era, together with a coracle on display. Great views over the estuary. Food available.

White Hart Inn, Finch St, St Dogmael's, Cardigan (01239 612099)

A long term survivor of the many pubs that once served St Dogmael's the White Hart has been pulling pints since at least the 1850s, when in the hands of a master mariner. The inn remained in the family's hands until well into the 1940s. Welcoming fireplace for the cold days, outside seating to the front for the hot days. Food available. Open all day, dogs welcome.

HISTORY NOTES
1. St Dogmael's (*Llandudoch*)

River Teifi at the Moorings, St Dogmael's

St Dogmael (or Dogfael) is believed to be the 6th century grandson of Prince Ceredig, who gave his name to Ceredigion, the Welsh name for the county of Cardigan. There are dedications to St Dogmael in Brittany and Anglesey. Evidence from Christian crosses found near the medieval abbey, and from early writings, suggest that his settlement was a Celtic monastery, either at the abbey's site, or else close by. The Welsh name for the village, Llandudoch, may derive from an unknown saint to whom an early church may have been dedicated, possibly there was another dedication to St Dogmael. Along with St David's and other monastic churches along the Welsh coast Llandudoch was attacked and sacked by the Norse in 988.

By the 12th century the old Welsh hundred of Cemais, roughly covering a large part of the Preseli area, was under the not entirely secure overlordship of the Norman fitz Martin family, who ruled from first their castle at Nevern, and then from Newport. Following conquest came piety and it was the Norman habit to follow conquest with the establishment of a place of worship. The established Celtic monasteries with their own unique customs were not to the new lords' liking, and with the newly reformed French orders in mind Robert fitz Martin chose to establish a monastery based on one of these new orders. In 1113 he visited the mother abbey of Tiron in France, returning with thirteen monks and a prior. Some five years later he visited Tiron again, returning with another thirteen monks and permission to raise the priory to an abbey, which appears to have been formally accomplished in 1120. At around the same time a Benedictine priory was founded at Cardigan. The abbey was well endowed by fitz Martin with lands in Pembrokeshire as well as further afield in Devon. His mother gave Caldey island, it's monastery becoming a dependent priory. The late 12th century saw the establishment of two other priories, at Pill near Milford Haven, and another in county Wexford, Ireland. The Tironian order had been established for those who desired a stricter interpretation of the rule of St Benedict, with a greater emphasis on manual labour and an insistence that a monk should be a skilled craftsman. Tironian monks initially wore a grey habit, later changing it to black. Whilst the order had nearly a hundred foundations in France, it's success in Britain was limited, and whilst there were abbeys in Scotland St Dogmael's was it's only abbey in England and Wales. Fortunes varied for the abbey, at one time it gained a reputation for licentiousness, and, despite improvements, by the time of the Dissolution in 1536 the abbey was a poor reflection of it's founders' aspirations. Still discernible from it's first phase of building, during the first half of the 12th century, are parts of the east and west range, and areas of the abbey church. Other remains survive from a number of modifications and rebuilding – there was a major rebuilding programme in the 14th century, possibly required because of damage during the Edwardian conquest of Wales. The present church of St Thomas the Martyr dates from 1847, with abbey materials on site being utilised for the building of the vicarage and coach house in 1866. The church houses the Sagranus stone, dating from the 6th century, and inscribed in both the Latin and Ogham alphabets (Ogham an Irish alphabet using cut lines to indicate letters) with a dedication to *Sagranus, son of Cunotamus*, a local chieftain.

By the late medieval period a settlement had developed outside the abbey, with an established market. The monks had rights to a fishery on the Teifi, and there are early references to salmon fishing and to Seine net fishing. By the 18th century St Dogmael's had developed into an important herring fishery, and by the late 19th century, with the help of trade along the Teifi to neighbouring Cardigan, the village had grown. At the heart of it's economy was the fishing for salmon and sea trout, or sewin, in spring and summer, herring in autumn and winter. Widely used around Britain, particularly in estuaries, seine net fishing involves the use of a plain wall of netting which is rowed out (nowadays an outboard motor is used) from shore on a semi-circular course, whilst one of the crew remains ashore holding a rope attached to one end of the net. Once the net is taut the boat returns to shore and the net hauled in. Most of the village's pre 20th century housing stock dates from the 19th century onwards, with modern housing tending to the periphery. One distinctive, and attractive, feature of some of the houses are alternate bandings of Teifi slate and brown stone. The village, or at least parts of it, were at different times either part of Pembrokeshire or Ceredigion, and in the days when Ceredigion was dry on a Sunday (ie the pubs were shut) the Pembrokeshire pubs did good business. In 2003 the village as a whole was finally settled in Pembrokeshire.

2. Poppit Sands

Poppit is one of Pembrokeshire's most popular beaches, good sand backed by sand dunes. Safe bathing inshore in the centre of the beach or where lifeguards indicate. The entrance to the river Teifi can be hazardous for vessels entering the estuary at certain states of the tide, and the estuary bar, a shifting sandbank, is known locally as the Cardigan bar. Cardigan's lifeboat station is at Poppit, equipped with two inshore lifeboats suitable for both the estuary and the rocky cliffs of the coast. The Teifi rises at Teifi Pools, on the Cambrian Mountains in mid Wales, running down to the sea through gorges and flat marshy areas. Cardigan island is a nature reserve in the hands of the Wildlife Trust of South and West Wales, home to seabirds and grazed by a herd of soay sheep. Restricted access. Cardigan Bay is home to one of the very few resident Atlantic bottlenose dolphin pods in the UK; the local beaches and boats can provide good siting opportunities.

WALK DIRECTIONS [-] indicates history note

1.   Starting from the parking area at the Moorings walk towards St Dogmael's [1] to shortly pass the Ferry Inn on your left. There is a footpath signposted to the left through the Ferry Inn grounds, but this leads only to the jetty at the inn. Continue past the inn, to shortly bear left onto a signposted path – just past a house called *The Old Bakery*, currently painted pink.

2.   Continue on the path above the river to reach the Green and the Teifi Netpool Inn. Follow the footpath around to the left of the Green. The Blessing Stone, in Welsh the *Carreg y Fendith*, where the Abbot blessed the fishing fleet, is signposted just off to the left before the picnic benches. The route onwards passes the standards on the left, wooden posts where the fishermen stretched out their nets, before descending to the river and the Pinog, where ships were built.

3.   Stay on the path, ignoring the walkway leading up to the town car park, until it swings inland to meet the main road through St Dogmael's. The path can be flooded at high tides, if so cross the green in front of the Netpool Inn and continue across the playing field to the town car park. Bear left from there to rejoin the route.

4.   Once at the main road bear right, continue past David Road, to turn left into Mill Street, opposite the

White Hart. Continue past the working mill to reach the abbey grounds and the Coach House. Go past the abbey ruins to reach a minor road. Bear right and continue ahead, ignoring roads leading off to the left.

5.   Shortly bear right onto a narrow path and passing a house named *Abbey Forge* on your left cross a footbridge and ascend to meet a minor road. Bear right. Continue uphill. Just before the road begins to go downhill bear sharp left onto a residential road at a No Through Road sign. Continue past the houses to reach a signposted footpath. Continue ahead – be aware of the sharp drop to your left. This is the cliff edge above Cwm Degwel ravine, the ravine created by glacial meltwater.

6.   Continue to reach a waymarked post and bear right through a kissing gate into a field. Keep to the right edge to meet another gate giving access to a green lane. Stay ahead, ignoring a path leading off up steps on the right, to reach a field. Continue initially ahead and then bearing around to the right reach the farm track leading to Pencnwc farm on your right. Stay on the track to reach a minor road.

7.   Bear left. Shortly bear right onto an open path – footpath sign by a telegraph pole here. Follow the path around to the left, and at a metal gate bear right to meet a farm gate. Go ahead across the field ahead, keeping to the right edge all the way round to meet a green lane. Follow the lane to reach the track leading to Bryncws farm. Bear right and follow the track to the road.

8.   Bear left and continue, leaving the road and taking a signposted bridleway leading off on the right at a bend in the road. Continue ahead to reach a crossroads of

paths and tracks. Bear right onto another bridleway and follow this to reach a large open field. Go ahead on a clear path as it descends to the farm of Manian-fawr.

9. Bear left. Shortly leave the track and bear right through a metal gate, almost immediately bearing left. Continue, to leave this path though a kissing gate on the right, and follow this new path as it bears around right, passing a caravan park on your left. Go ahead to reach the caravan park itself.

10. Continue ahead towards buildings. Bear right – there is a big sign here pointing right stating Beach. Keeping the buildings on your left follow the path onwards and around to the left to reach a minor road. Bear right to reach the beach and the road from Poppit Sands [2] to St Dogmael's.

11. Bear right onto the St Dogmael's road and follow it back to the starting point. There are two small paths off to the left running alongside the road before the Webley hotel is reached. Short uphill section just after the Webley hotel, otherwise on the level.

FACILITIES

Local producers' market held at the Coach House, the visitor's centre and café to the abbey, every Tuesday 09.00 to 13.00. Adjacent to the abbey is Y Felin (*The Mill*), one of Wales' last working mills, producing stone ground flour. Café at Poppit Sands. St Dogmael's marks the start (or finish) of the Pembrokeshire Coast Path, some 186 miles/299 kilometres in length, ending at Amroth on the south coast. There is a plaque at the Moorings noting it's start, as well as a carving of a mermaid, who advised one local St Dogmael's fisherman of weather conditions after he had released her after capture in his nets.

2. CILGERRAN

4 miles/6.5 kilometres

OS Maps: 1:25 000 North Pembrokeshire Outdoor Leisure 35, 1:25 000 Newcastle Emlyn/Castell Newydd Emlyn Explorer 185.
Start: Cardiff Arms in Cilgerran's main street – close to the turning to the castle.
Access: Cilgerran is easily reached from the A478 Cardigan to Crymych road. Bus 430 stops at Cilgerran, en route from Cardigan to Crymych and Narberth Monday to Saturday, 431 Cardigan to Pentre Galar Fridays only, and 230 Cardigan to Carmarthen first Wednesday every month.
Parking: Small parking area opposite the Cardiff Arms. Parking also possible at the Cilgerran Coracle Centre – follow the road down to the river from Cilgerran's main street, public toilets here.
Grade: Easy.

Cardiff Arms, High St, Cilgerran (01239 614600) So named because it's first landlord hailed originally from Cardiff it is believed that it was built in anticipation of the arrival of the railway, however when it came the station was built at the other end of the village. The pub has hanging outside a fishing coracle, much in favour by local fishermen at one time for catching sewin and salmon. Beer garden to rear. Food available.

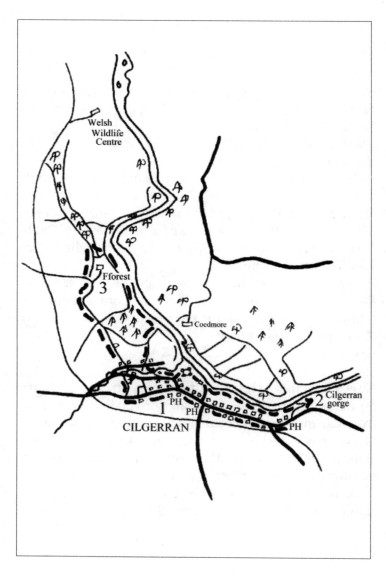

Welsh
Wildlife
Centre

Fforest

3

Coedmore

1   PH
PH

2 Cilgerran
gorge

CILGERRAN   PH

Pendre Inn, High St, Cilgerran (01239 614223)
Dating back to the 14th century the interior features slate floors, old beams and an inglenook fireplace, together with lots of memorabilia. At one time the area to the front of the inn hosted a splendid old ash tree, but in 2008 it's trunk was found to be hollow and it had to be demolished. Garden area.

Masons' Arms, Cnwce (07989 990461)
The sharp hairpin slope down to the river by the side of the pub served as a ramp to carry slate up from the river quarries to the village above – hence the Masons' Arms local name of the Ramp or Rampin. The pub's opening dates back to the area's heyday as a slate quarrying centre. Garden area to front.

HISTORY NOTES
1. Cilgerran
There may have been a village here, clustered around the 6th century church, but written records date the village from the early 13th century, with the town growing up around the Norman castle. The town became noted for it's great cattle fairs, with two summer fairs held by 1800. 1800 was a good year for Cilgerran, a total of twenty thousand beasts were sold. Wool was another strong seller, with cargoes taken down to Cardigan from 1600 onwards for sale, particularly to men from North Wales, who wove the wool into suitable clothes for sale in Shrewsbury. With the 19th century slate quarrying came to the fore, and the town took on the aspect of a quarrymen's village.

The church is dedicated to St Llawddog, a 6th

century hermit who is believed to have rejected a kingdom – his father was the King of Usk – in favour of a life of contemplation. His example gathered followers, and 6th century churches were dedicated to him here and at nearby Cenarth. The present church can be traced back to the 13th century; the tall Norman tower would have acted as a lookout and extra line of defence for those who could not reach the safety of the castle. However the building had fallen into such a poor state of repair by the mid 19th century that in 1855 the whole building, excepting the 13th century tower, was completely rebuilt. There is an ogham stone in the ground, inscribed in Latin and ogham, and dedicated to *Trenegussus, the son of Macutrenus*, who died in the 6th century. Looking much like a worn stone pillar it is amongst the gravestones to the left of the path leading from the church to the main Cilgerran road. Ogham was a script, invented in Ireland by the 5th century, which uses groups of lines to represent Goidelic, the old Irish tongue. Ogham stones are fairly common in Pembrokeshire, and tend to mark the grave of a chieftain. They also provide evidence of strong Irish ties with Pembrokeshire and the west in the 5th to 7th centuries.

NEST, THE HELEN OF WALES

It was Gerald of Windsor who founded the first castle in Cilgerran, Cenarth Bychan, probably in 1108, and probably on the site of the present castle. Gerald was something of a Norman adventurer, who had been given the custody of Pembroke castle in 1102 after successful defence of it against the Welsh in 1096. He built a second castle on land at Carew, which he gained as part of the dowry of his new wife Nest, the daughter of Rhys ap Tewdwr, the ruler of the old kingship of Deheubarth (south-west Wales). Nest was well famed for her beauty, and Gerald no doubt felt he was well favoured. Seeking to consolidate his claim to Welsh lands he had chosen his new site with his eyes across the Teifi to Ceredigion. However Gerald was not without enemies, nor Nest without her admirers.

In 1109 Nest's second cousing Owain ap Cadwgan, who also had claims on Ceredigion, paid Nest a visit as a kinsman in her and Gerald's newly fortified castle. Events were later chronicled in the medieval *Chronicle of the Princes*, for Owain returned later that night with a small retinue of men, surrounded Gerald and Nest's bedchamber, and began to set fire to the buildings, with the intention of burning them alive. Nest advised Gerald to escape by the privy hole adjacent to the chamber, which he speedily did. Nest then called out that Gerald had escaped, and she and her children – one Angharad, was to become the mother of Giraldus Cambrensis, Gerald of Wales, whose descriptions of Wales and Ireland remain in print – were seized by Owain. She is reputed to have told him that if her children were returned to their father she would stay with Owain; it is also reputedly said that she was perfectly willing to comply with this idea. Owain may also have thought himself fortunate, but Nest was no demure princess, and a series of further amorous adventures were to follow, including for a time, her becoming the mistress of the King, Henry I.

Her abduction, her beauty, and her number of lovers and children gained her notoriety, and she gained herself the title of *Helen of Wales.*

Cilgerran castle

In the later Norman era an agreement was made between William 1, a visitor to St David's in 1081, and Rhys ap Tewdwr, ruler of Deheubarth (present day Pembrokeshire, Carmarthenshire, Ceredigion and the Gower), that for £40 a year Rhys could continue to rule southern Wales. However with the death of William in 1087, and Rhys in 1093, it was open day. Earl Roger of Shrewsbury marched as far as Cardigan, where he built a castle, before moving south where his son established the lordship of Pembroke. Pembroke castle was eventually given to Gerald of Windsor in 1102, and it was he who crossed the Preseli hills to establish Cenarth Bychan on what is probably the site of the present castle. Ownership of the castle then passed to alternate attacking Welsh and Normans before a more permanent Norman castle was built by William Marshal the younger in 1223. To William's original drum tower a second was added some years later, which together with strong defensive walls, made it one of the most imposing castles of Wales. Alternatively in disrepair and rebuilt, the castle was by the 18th century a Romantic ruin. Boat trips from Cardigan carried 18th and 19th century tourists and artists upriver to view the castle, perched as bright as the Romantic imagination on it's rocky crag; among the artists Richard Wilson, Peter de Wint and JMW Turner left their impressions.

2. Cilgerran gorge

Cilgerran gorge, the longest of the Teifi river gorges, is just over three miles / five kilometres long, and owes it's splendid deep isolation to cutting of the rocks during the Ice Age. The original course lay to the west, along the bed of the present tiny river Piliau. The great Irish Sea glacier is believed to have blocked the original course, leaving the Teifi to cut anew. Downriver, at Cardigan, the estuary has formed an extensive saltmarsh. The building of the Cardi Bach railway in 1885, from

Cardigan to Whitland, had the effect of dividing the saltmarsh in two; the result being a freshwater marsh to one side, and a saltmarsh on the other. The railway itself closed in 1963. The Wildlife Trust of South and West Wales has established the Welsh Wildlife Centre here, noting the area as *without doubt one of the finest wetland reserves in the Principality* ... Well worth the visit for the variety of habitats and wildlife on display – the otter a frequent visitor. Water buffalo are currently being used to help clear vegetation, and open up areas of greater open water.

Cilgerran gorge

The river is tidal to just below Cilgerran, and is home to not just the otter but also sea trout (sewin) and salmon, the salmon returning to spawn in the creeks where they were born. The salmon do not always travel alone, for seals follow, and have been seen as far as Cenarth falls, twelve and a half miles / twenty kilometres from the sea. That other predator, man, has made a living here, fishing from coracles made from local willow, hazel and ash, with skins of hide or calico. Cilgerran, along with other Teifi valley villages of Llechryd, Abercych and Cenarth, was famed as a centre of coracle fishing, and the four villages' sections of the river were fished according to strict protocols. The technique is to stretch a net between two coracles – the net being held by hand. At one time a net across the river was connected to a bell at Coedmore, the mansion above the river. Medieval Cilgerran had a salmon weir below the castle, with six traps, and was rated the finest weir in Wales. A later salmon and sewin weir, below Llechryd's fine stone bridge two miles / three kilometres upstream, was smashed by Rebecca rioters in 1843 in protest at turnpike tolls and at interference with local fishermen's livelihood.

The gorge's industrial heyday was during the 19th century. It was littered with slate tips and the quays and towpaths where the barges were loaded with slate for transport down river to Cardigan. There was even a narrow gauge railway downstream to help trundle away the slate waste, built in response to concerns raised in 1850 about the impact on fishing and the environment of the practice of dumping quarry rubbish in the river Teifi. By 1860 five quarries at least were active, with many quarrymen brought down from North Wales for their expertise, yet by 1891 quarrying had been abandoned. The best slate was exchanged for cargoes of limestone and coal dust (required for mixing with clay to make culm bricks, placed in kilns with the lime to make fertilizer) brought in by ketch from south Pembrokeshire and South Wales. These were cargoes of *sea slate*, suitable for billiard tables, roofing and floors, whilst the poorer *land slate* was sold locally, often for similar purposes. Some of the local slate was used in restoration work on the church, on village buildings, and as tombstones in the churchyard. In it's heyday the quarry employed some three hundred men, which together with the tinplate works at nearby Llechryd, made the area a hive of industrial enterprise. The remains of the slate industry are still here, re-colonised by nature.

3. Fforest
The woodland along this stretch of the Teifi is typical of the wooded slopes of the gorge, with oaks, ash and wild service trees protected from excessive felling by the steepness of the incline. Fforest farm, a former manor house, was home to Dr Thomas Phaer, physician to Mary 1 and translator of Virgil's Aeneid. He died in 1560.

WALK DIRECTIONS [-] indicates history note
1. Starting from the Cardiff Arms follow the road through Cilgerran **[1]** to the Masons' Arms in neighbouring Cnwce. Immediately adjacent to the pub is a footpath, signposted, leading downhill right, through woodland, then turning sharp left to meet the river through Cilgerran gorge **[2]**. Follow the track bearing left to reach the Coracle Centre.
2. Continue past the Coracle Centre and follow the directions for *Castle and Village* – there is a path left just past the Centre leading up via steps. The *Riverside Walk* leads to a small slate stone beach below the castle.

Continue uphill, ignore a path leading off to the right, and where a path is met bear left and keeping the castle walls on your right follow the path around to reach the castle entrance.

3. Once by the castle entrance turn left and then right (left would take you back to the start!) onto the road leading to the church. Just past *Ger Y Llan* – a residential street on the left – there is a footpath right, indicated by a metal sign of a walking man. Follow the footpath downhill to cross a stream, and continue right, in front of houses, turning left uphill to meet a minor road.

4. Turn left onto the minor road, and passing a house and garage, turn right over a stile into a field. Walking man signpost here. Keeping to the right field edge cross to meet a stile giving access to a pine wood. Follow the path as it turns initially right, and then left, as it follows the course of the wooded Teifi gorge. Good views of the river below.

5. Continue through woodland to the stile at Fforest [3]. Ignore the waymark indicating a right turn; instead cross the path, and continuing straight ahead on a permissive path follow it downhill right – ignore paths off to left and right – to reach an old quarry on the right. Ignore the path leading off to the right ahead, instead turn sharp left onto a wooded path.

6. Continue on the wooded path to meet another quarry on the left just past a stile. Keep ahead and follow the path track around it to reach a road track leading to Fforest. Turn right and follow the track as it bears left and ahead to a tarmac road. At the tarmac road turn left,

and then immediately right, descend down stone steps to cross a stream by a concrete footbridge, and then ascend to another tarmac road.

7.   Turn left and walk uphill to shortly turn right into Cilgerran church. Follow the path through the church grounds, and continue on a path to meet the main road through Cilgerran. Bear left and continue through the village to reach the starting point.

FACILITIES

Most facilities available in Cilgerran. Public toilets at the Coracle Centre, en route. The Welsh Wildlife Centre, just to the north of the village, is highly recommended – canoe trips on the Teifi run from here. Part of the old Cardi Bach rail line is used as a National Cycle trail, the route leading along the road from Cilgerran to the Wildlife Centre, and then on to Cardigan. Fforest farm and camp offer up market camping.

3. ABERCYCh

3.75 miles/6 kilometres

OS Maps: 1:25 000 Newcastle Emlyn/Castell Newydd Emlyn Explorer 185.
Start: The Nag's Head in Abercych.
Access: Abercych itself is just off the B4332 Boncath and Newchapel to Cenarth road; the Nag's Head just off this road after Abercych village, before the road crosses the bridge at Pontseli and heads on to Cenarth. Bus 431 Cardigan to Cilgerran, Newchapel and Boncath stops at Abercych Fridays only.
Parking: Parking on the minor road by the Nag's Head.
Grade: Easy.

The Nag's Head, Abercych (01239 841200)
An attractive inn overlooking the river Cych there has been an inn here since the early 19th century, though it's origins may date back to the 1780s. Doubling up during it's early history as the local smithy one late 19th century landlord, Josiah Evans, has been credited with the invention of an iron plough which gained favour in America and Australia. One long term resident of the pub since the 1950s has been the Giant Rat of Abercych. Now stuffed and on display the 'rat' had been sighted for several months roaming the Cych valley, and there were fears that this might herald a new breed of super rat, something along the lines of Sherlock Holmes' famous Giant Rat of Sumatra. Cornered one evening by the then landlord David Morris it was killed with the fork he was

69

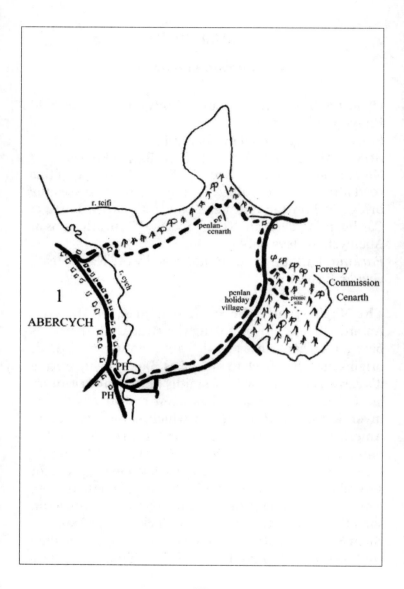

r. teifi

penlan-
cenarth

1

ABERCYCH

r. cych

penlan
holiday
village

picnic
site

Forestry
Commission
Cenarth

PH

PH

using to dig up potatoes. The rat was later identified as an escaped coypu. Until the early 1990s the inn had been fairly small, but it's new landlord bought up the neighboring shop and workshop and the inn now occupies the whole terrace. The Biblical quotation on both sides of the pub sign translates as *be wise as a serpent, harmless as a dove*. Brewed off site it offers it's own Emrys ale. Restaurant and bar area, and garden by the river.

The Nag's Head

Penrhiw Inn, Abercych (01239 682229)
Dating back to the 1860s the original Penrhiw was sited opposite the present inn on the other side of the road, but owing to it's position at the dangerous corner

downhill to Pontseli it was demolished in the mid 1970s to improve visibility. It's licence was transferred to the old Post Office and shop. The old inn now forms the hardcore for the present inn's car park.

HISTORY NOTES
1. Abercych
The village takes it's name from the river Cych which runs into the river Teifi here from it's source some eight miles / thirteen kilometres to the south east. At one time there was just Forge Cych at the bottom of the valley close to the Teifi, and workers houses grew up in it's shadow. The forge has gone now but the village, really an amalgam of several hamlets, has continued it's pattern of linear development from the 19th century until now. It's houses by necessity accommodate the valley slopes by either cutting into the slope, or jutting out over the valley. The valley itself forms the boundary between Pembrokeshire and Carmarthenshire. Cych valley (*Glyn Cuch*) features in the medieval Welsh tales of the Mabinogion, one of the masterpieces of European literature. In the first tale, Pwyll was out hunting in the valley, following his dogs, when he heard the cries of another pack coming towards his own. As his dogs reached an open clearing Pwyll could see this other pack pursuing and bringing down a stag. No ordinary dogs for *the colour that was on them was a brilliant shining white, and their ears red; and as the exceeding whiteness of the dogs glittered, so glittered the exceeding redness of their ears*. Pwyll drove them away and baited his own pack upon the stag. As he did so a

72

horseman approached him and asked Pwyll to explain his discourtesy in driving away the pack that had killed the stag and setting his own on it. The horseman and owner of the pack was Arawn king of Annwn, the Otherworld, a world of delights and eternal youth, and whose location, it was implied in the tale, was in Dyfed – the Cych valley perhaps being one of it's entrances. To make amends for his insult Pwyll agreed to change places with Arawn for a year and a day, and to slay Arawn's enemy King Hafgan, also a king with his own kingdom in Annwn. At the end of the agreed time Pwyll returned to Glyn Cuch to meet with Arawn. Hafgan had been slain and the two kingdoms united under one crown. This, and Pwyll's chaste behaviour towards Arawn's wife, gained Arawn's friendship and Pwyll from then on became known as Pwyll Head of Annwn. The valley remains secluded and well wooded, it's steep sides it's protection from agriculture. Until well into the 1930s the village was noted for the quality of it's woodland craftsmanship, it's bowl turning and carved spoons, but with mass production and lack of apprentices came the end of the craft. The bridge over the river Cych at Pontseli is very similar to that at Cenarth in that it has openings set into the structure. Here it has two openings, the theory being that not only do these openings reduce the weight of masonry, but they also reduce water pressure during floods. It may have been build by William Edwards who built the bridge at Cenarth, and may date from the same time in the 18th century.

WALK DIRECTIONS [-] indicates history note

1.   Starting from the Nag's Head walk up the hill away from the bridge, bear right, and continue through the attractive village of Abercych **[1]**. Just past the Post Office and old school bear right onto a No Through Road at a house marked *Glynwell*.

2.   Continue downhill to bear right through a kissing gate at the ford – the ford is a popular local spot in the hot summer days. Continue over a footbridge, and ignoring the track leading off to the right continue on the track ahead. Keeping the house on your right follow the track as it bears right around it.

3.   At a fork bear right and follow the track as it bears uphill. Continue until where the track meets a junction of paths at a farm gate bear left – right leads on to Penlan-Cenarth. Shortly bear sharp right – the road ahead left is a Private Road. Continue downhill to reach the main road.

4.   Bear right – left would take you on to Cenarth – and continue to reach the Forestry Commission's site *Cenarth* on your left – a small mixed species woodland. Bear left into the site, and just past the fence on your left bear left and join a short circular path as it bears uphill and around right to reach a picnic site. There is a longer circular walk leading off from the parking/turning area just past the picnic site – this would add ½ mile/¾ kilometre or so to the walk. Can be muddy.

5.   From the Forestry site bear left back onto the main road and continue on to reach the Nag's Head and the starting point.

FACILITIES

Just behind the Nag's Head is Clynfyw, offering woodland paths and a sculpture trail – notice board at entrance. Access on the public footpath just to the left of the pub. Post Office currently open Monday and Thursday mornings. Penlan Holiday Village is passed en route.

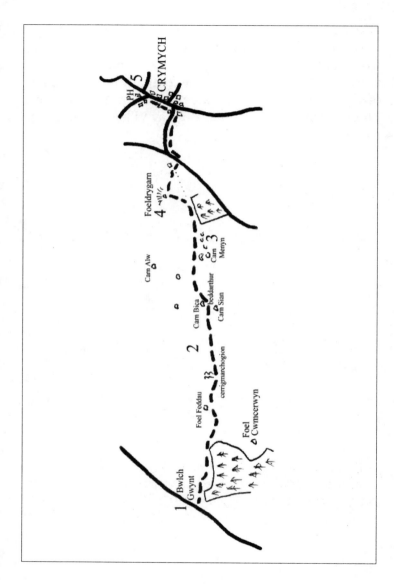

4. the Golden Road

8.75 miles/14 kilometres

OS Maps: 1:25 000 North Pembrokeshire Outdoor Leisure 35.

Start: Bwlch Gwynt.

Access: Bwlch Gwynt can be found on the main road across the Preseli hills – the B4329. It is marked on the OS map. There is a summer (July to September) Preseli Hills Bus which runs between Bwlch Gwynt and Crymych (and vice versa). Current contact number for details and times is 0800 783 1584, or contact Tourist Information Centres.

Parking: Rough parking possible at the start point.

Grade: Strenuous.

Crymych Arms Inn, Crymych (01239 831435)

The inn's written history dates back to the 1861 census, though a building on site, which may then have been a farm, is shown on an earlier 1812 map. It's position was at the meeting point of six roads, which then was a collection and meeting point for cattle drovers. One major reason for the inn's establishment was in order to cater for them, particularly during fair time. Another was it's siting on the Cardigan to Narberth coach route. Until the arrival of the railway here in July 1874 there was little to identify the place as a village, indeed the Crymych Arms gave it's name, Crymych, to the railway halt, and then to the town that grew up here.

HISTORY NOTES
1. Bwlch Gwynt and the Golden Road
Bwlch Gwynt – the windy pass – stands at the highest point of the mountain road from north to south Pembrokeshire, and is a popular and convenient starting point for exploration of the Preseli hills. The route follows part of the Golden Road across the Preseli hills to the great Bronze Age cairn of Foel Drygarn. The description golden refers to the route's use during the Bronze Age as a trade route and trackway from Wessex in south-west England, to Whitesands Bay, near St David's, and Ireland, where goods, possibly locally made Preseli stone axes, were traded for copper and gold from the Wicklow hills. The track has had many names – the Pilgrim's Way, the Roman Road, the Robbers' Road. It was also known as the Flemings' Way, for the simple reason that Flemish settlers brought into the county by colonising Normans found it safer to take to the tops, out of the way of ambushing Welsh. Thousands of cattle, sheep and pigs, even geese, with their drovers, would have used the route, particularly with the coming of toll gates to the plains, stamping out a path across the hills. Nowadays the hills are common land, grazed by the mountain ponies and the sheep during the better weather.

2. Bwlch Gwynt to Carn Menyn
The Preseli hills as we see them today are the remnants of a mountain chain thrown up during the Caledonian orogeny of four hundred million years ago – a mountain range that stretched from Britain to Scandinavia. The high cairns are made of harder igneous rock than the softer surrounding sedimentary and metamorphic rocks.

Carn Bica, a typical Preseli cairn, may once have been used as a Bronze Age burial mound, but the stones have been much disturbed. Just below, to the right, is Beddarthur, the grave of King Arthur (one of many), the small stones delineating a grave of suitable size for so large a hero – however originally this may have been a Neolithic burial mound. At Carn Sian, Jane's Cairn, there is said to have been a chapel at some time in it's history, though no ruins survive. There is a plaque near Carn Sian, unveiled in 1984, in memory of a Liberator which crashed here in September 1944, killing five of the nine man crew. Grid reference OS 127322.

To the north-east of Carn Bica, sited on Preseli's northern slope and off the route of the main walk, is Carn Alw, which has evidence of an Iron Age hillfort dating from the late first millennium BC. Utilising outcropping rock within it's rampart it's most distinctive feature is a *chevaux de frise* on it's west side. Rare in Britain a *chevaux de frise* is a defensive device whereby small stones are set upright in the ground by a defensive weakness. Here there are thousands of small stones up to a metre in height set in an arc of three separate bands around the entrance. Lack of evidence for habitation has led to speculation that the site may have been a base for summer upland grazing or as a refuge in case of attack. There is evidence of houses and cleared fields in the vicinity of Carn Alw, and there would have been permanent settlements to the north on lower ground. There may have been an earlier Bronze Age agricultural settlement to the south. Carn Alw is also unusual in that it is made of rhyolite, unlike the other outcrops in the eastern area of the Preseli which are of dolerite.

3. Carn Menyn

Carn Menyn, or Carn Meini, lays claim to fame as the source for the bluestones of Stonehenge. It was in the early 1920s that the geologist H. H. Thomas discovered that many of the bluestones from the inner circle came from Carn Menyn. From this discovery grew the theory that Neolithic peoples transported over eighty stones, with a weight of over 250 tons, from one sacred site on the Preseli hills to another at Stonehenge, a distance of approximately 180 miles/290 kilometres. In the 1950s the BBC proved that such a feat was possible, using river and land transport. This popular theory is countered by the suggestion that the Irish Sea glacier, which at least once in it's history spread as far as Somerset and Avon, transported the stones there in their icy progress, and that when Stonehenge was built these stones were chosen as the most suitable. A medieval theory had Merlin as the magical agent, moving the stones with their healing properties from the so called Giant's Dance in Ireland when all others had failed to move them, and re-erecting them on their present site with the help of a giant. Recent excavations at Stonehenge in 2008 have led to the idea that fifty six bluestones formed a ring 285 feet/87 metres across as early as 3000 BC, thus making this the earliest stone structure known. These stones were then moved to the inner circle in 2300 BC. There is at Carn Menyn a flat slab, cut as if ready for transport, and known as the altar stone; this may be all that is left of a small Neolithic burial chamber. No doubt many of the rocks owe their shape to shattering by frost, when the ground was frozen solid during the Ice Age. In April 1989 a bluestone pillar from here was flown down by helicopter and set up at Rhos Fach, on the minor road leading out from Mynachlog Ddu, whilst a twin was flown on to Stonehenge to act as a marker for the origin of the bluestones.

Carn Menyn

OF WILD BOARS AND KINGS

In that superb book of medieval Welsh tales, the Mabinogion, the story of Culwch and Olwen relates the royal hunt of Arthur in the chase of the magic boar, Twrch Trwyth. Culwch, in love with Olwen, had requested her hand, but with a giant as a prospective father in law things were never going to be easy. Ysbaddan Giant required, among other items, the comb and shears from between the ears of Twrch Trwyth, with which his *hair may be dressed, so exceeding stiff it is*. Undaunted Culwch enlisted the help of his cousin, Arthur.

The hunt began in Ireland, where Twrch Trwyth, a former king who for his wickedness had been turned into a swine, was laying waste the country. Pursued by Arthur and his knights, Twrch Trwyth crossed to Wales, landing at Porth Clais near St David's. The magic boar then proceeded to slaughter men and cattle on his way across St David's peninsula to Foel Cwmcerwyn in the Preseli hills. There, on Preseli ridge, many of Arthur's knights were slain, their bodies turning instantly to stone. Cerrigmarchogion, the Knights' Stones, marks the spot.

Twrch Trwyth was finally driven into the Severn estuary and on into Cornwall, where the comb and shears were taken from him. Culwch duly gained his reward, Twrch Trwyth, however, escaped into the sea. So if you see any wild boar on your walks – you have been warned!

4. Foeldrygarn

Foeldrygarn, the hill of the three cairns, is the most spectacular of the Bronze Age cairns that dot the Preseli hills. It's siting, as with other Preseli Bronze Age cairns, is probably associated with the hill's use as a trackway. Unlike Neolithic burial mounds, whose structure allowed for multiple burials, the Bronze Age cairns were built for a single occupant. It's strategic position proved ideal to later Iron Age people who built a large hillfort, incorporating the burial mounds within it. It had three defended enclosures. There is evidence of occupation from the first millennium BC to early first millennium AD, with indication of seventy seven platforms in the main inner enclosure, sixty three in the middle, and a further number in the annexe and outer area. Occupation would likely have been spread over different time periods. Gaps in the remaining walls may well be the original entrances.

5. Crymych

Originally a collection point for cattle droves Crymych in the early 1800s was just a few farms and houses then known as Iet y Bwlch (gate of the pass). The name by which the town and inn became known is an old one dating back to the 1460s, though it has had a number of spellings. One translation of it in it's present spelling is *crym*, meaning hunched up, and *ych* ox. The development of the town began with the arrival of the *Cardi Bach* railway (officially the Whitland and Taf Vale Railway) in July 1874. Begun in Whitland in November 1870 the 27½ mile long railway finally reached it's destination at Cardigan in September 1886. Originally constructed to carry local slate and lead ore it was agricultural products that proved it's mainstay. Market and mart grew rapidly, and new businesses and trades moved into the village. By the late 1880s the number of annual fairs had increased to twelve, including hiring fairs. Many of Crymych's new buildings added verandas for customers to tie up their horses, giving it the appearance of an Australian or Wild West country town; locally it became known as *Cowboy Town*. The railway closed in 1963, it's route still traceable in places. The town is still an important agricultural centre for the area, as it is culturally and educationally – the main comprehensive school for the Preseli area opened in the town in 1958, and *Ysgol Y Preseli* has been designated a bilingual school since 1991, science and English are taught predominantly through the medium of English, other subjects through the medium of Welsh.

WALK DIRECTIONS [-] indicates history note

1.   Starting from Bwlch Gwynt [1] take the obvious path heading out across the hills, keeping initially a fence, and then Pantmaenog Forest, to your right. Where the forestry ends there is access right up to open moorland and on to Preseli's highest point, Foel Cwmcerwyn. The Golden Road itself continues straight ahead, diverting to include Foel Cwmcerwyn will add well over a mile/1½ kilometres to the walk – walk 5, Rosebush and Preseli Top, incorporates Foel Cwmcerwyn in it's route.

2.   Continue on the Golden Road to Foel Feddau and it's Bronze Age cairn, and through the broken rocks of Cerrigmarchogion (the rocks of the knights). Continuing on the route is crossed by the deeply rutted tracks of the old north to south drover's road. Utilising the dip in the ridge the track led south from Eglwyswrw to Mynachlog Ddu and Maenclochog.

3.   Continue on the clearly defined track to Carn Bica and Beddarthur [2], and follow it on to Carn Menyn [3].

From Carn Menyn follow the path as it skirts the forestry plantation on the right. There are paths on the left en route which will lead up to the summit of Foeldrygarn **[4]**, an easy one (and usually a little drier) leads off left just after the forestry ends.

4. From Foeldrygarn descend to the far corner where it abuts farmland and reach gate and stile. Cross and either continue on the track ahead, or bear left and then right on another track, to reach a minor road. Bear left and follow the road as it bends right and continue to reach the T junction with the A487. Bear left and continue on into Crymych **[5]** – the Crymych Arms is at the far end of the town.

FACILITIES
All available in Crymych.

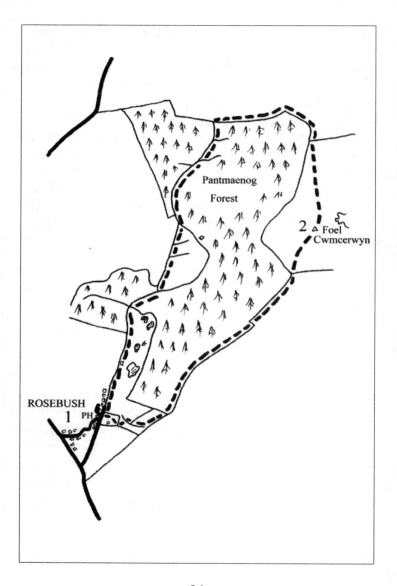

Pantmaenog Forest

2 △ Foel Cwmcerwyn

ROSEBUSH

1 PH

5. Rosebush and Preseli top

5 miles/8 kilometres

OS Maps: 1:25 000 North Pembrokeshire Outdoor Leisure 35.

Start: By the Tafarn Sinc in Rosebush.

Access: Rosebush can be reached from the B4313 Maenclochog to New Inn road. Buses 344 Fishguard to Haverfordwest Tuesdays only and 345 Mynachlog Ddu and Maenclochog to Fishguard Thursdays only. There is a summer (July to September) Preseli Hills Bus which calls at Rosebush Tuesdays, Thursdays and Saturdays – details, at time of writing, from 0800 783 1584, or contact Tourist Information Centres.

Parking: Tafarn Sinc has a car park for patrons – parking area in village also by a children's playground; go ahead on Rosebush's street, to bear left in front of the Old Post Office – signposted.

Grade: Strenuous.

Tafarn Sinc (01437 532214) www.tafarnsinc.com

Originally named the Precelly Hotel the inn was built in 1876 when the Maenclochog Railway from Clunderwen to Rosebush was inaugurated. Closed in 1992 it was bought locally and re-opened under it's present name; in English it translates as the *zinc tavern* and is made of timber walls and corrugated iron galvanized with zinc. Part of the old railway halt has been re-created, and the occasional sound of a simulated steam train echoes around the garden area. Inside the atmosphere is unique, with, as in the old farmhouse kitchens, hams hanging from the ceiling, and a sawdust floor, woodburning stoves, and cultural and photographic memorabilia around the walls. Real ale – the Cwrw Tafarn Sinc is brewed for the pub – and draught

beer, and locally produced food. Currently closed Mondays.

The Old Post Office (01437 532205)

Originally the quarry manger's house for the Rosebush quarry, and then the local Post Office and shop. Change of use in 1979 saw it re-open as a licensed bistro, restaurant and tea room. Cosy bar downstairs. Occasional music evenings. A popular walkers' stop with a patio area to the front.

HISTORY NOTES

1. Rosebush

The name Rosebush, whilst pretty, is probably an Anglicisation of the Welsh *Rhos y Bwlch*, moorland pass. At one time a settlement of four houses the village grew with the development of the slate quarries (both slab and roofing slate, and distinctively dark blue in colour) which were cut into a spur of Foel Cwmcerwyn, the Preseli hills highest point. Comprising Bellstone and Rosebush Quarries each had two major working areas.

Bellstone, to the north, was the first, and had been in operation certainly at some time in the 18th century. In 1825 it came under the management of a JF Barham, who had moved here from Craig y Cwm quarry, an unsuccessful quarry cut out of the eastern side of Foel Cwmcerwyn. Management of the quarry changed several times, with a name change in 1866 when the formerly named Prescelly Quarry became the Bellstone Slate Company. The 1870s and 1880s were it's most intensive period of operation, however by 1889 work had ceased. Spoil heaps remain, as does a deep drained pit. Quarry House is now occupied; some of the old outbuildings used for domestic purposes.

Preseli hills and Pantmaenog forest

Rosebush Quarry's early history is uncertain. Possibly worked in the early 1840s, a later 1860s venture to bring it into operation is known to have failed. In 1869 the freehold was bought by an Edward Cropper, an MP from Kent. He put his stepson, Joseph Macaulay, in charge, and new workings on four terraces were opened up. One new feature was indicative of grand ideas to come when a windmill was erected on the upper levels, probably to drive dressing machines. However before it's power could be utilised it was subject to storm damage; it's original site is now lost. To assist sales and slate transport Edward Cropper signed an agreement with the Great Western Railway (GWR) in 1871 to build a rail link from Clunderwen on the Pembrokeshire Carmarthenshire boundary to Rosebush, and in January 1876 the *Maenclochog Railway* opened for freight traffic, with passenger trains running from September of that year. 1877 saw 23,973½ passengers using the service (what constituted half a passenger wasn't specified), and income from them was only £250 or so behind the freight income of £782. Further rail developments were planned with the 1878 Act of Parliament authorising the *Rosebush* (later changed to *North Pembrokeshire*) *and Fishguard Railway*, planned to run from Rosebush on to Goodwick and a proposed Fishguard harbour link for Irish Sea ferry services. The development of the village dates from this period, with twenty six quarrymen's cottages being built along what is still known as *The Terrace*. Water to them was piped from a newly created quarry pool – water from the same pool was used to power quarry machinery and run the locos. The pool and pipe are still there, the pool normally a fine bluey green colour.

In 1877 Cropper died, his widow Margaret later marrying local landowner Colonel John Owen. They had been assisting Macaulay in the development of Rosebush, and to boost fortunes it was decided to promote Rosebush as a mountain resort. The Precelly hotel was built, gardens were laid out and planted with shrubs and trees, alongside artificial lakes. Embellishments included fountains and grottoes. A coach service to Fishguard was inaugurated, and stables built alongside the station. As a poster for the Maenclochog Railway put it Rosebush was *the place of all others for pleasure and picnic parties*. Colonel Owen had distinct views on the type of visitor he wished to attract; he is reported to have said of cyclists that *not one word can be said in favour of them. They cheat the nation, they defraud the Railway Companies of their fares, they bilk the turnpikes ... a pint of beer perhaps the only harvest of the town through which they pass*. However whatever type the visitor Rosebush failed to prosper as a spa, it's water had no distinct properties, and with a slump in slate prices the Maenclochog Railway closed in December 1882. Following better negotiated terms with the GWR the line re-opened in 1884 only to close four years later, with the line being put up for sale in 1889. The North Pembrokeshire and Fishguard Railway had run into trouble from the start, construction had begun in 1879 but by 1892 only a mile had been built. In that year with the acquisition of a controlling interest in the company by a Birmingham solicitor, prospects improved. The Maenclochog Railway was bought in 1894, and in 1895 the line re-opened from Clunderwen to Rosebush, and on to Letterston, with work being undertaken to extend the line to Goodwick. The line however did not prosper, and was eventually bought out by the GWR in 1898, who with their own links to Neyland and the Irish Sea would have viewed any link to Fishguard and Carmarthen by another company as unwanted competition. The link on to Fishguard was finally completed in 1899.

Slate as freight and commercial enterprise had effectively reached it's peak in the early 1880s and the quarry, which at it's peak had employed over a hundred men, was idle by the end of the decade. There were attempts to revive it, but when in 1908 both Rosebush and Bellstone quarries came up for sale and were bought no tenant could be found to work them. The rail line between Fishguard, Rosebush and Clunderwen continued mainly as a passenger service, surviving as such until 1937. It found a different use during the Second World War when empty railway carriages were used as target practice by the RAF. Maenclochog tunnel found use as a target for a new bouncing bomb; twelve dummy bombs were launched at it, one bounced around inside the tunnel and came out the other end. Observers included Barnes Wallis. The line was repaired, only to finally close in 1949. It is still possible to trace the course of the line. Quarry remains include the substantial walls of the mill building and the ruined loco shed opposite. The levels can still be walked; on the upper levels are the remains of the dressing sheds. Tunnels can still be discerned, level five's, just before the mill, has an attractive arch. The abutments for the bridge which crossed the railway line, once the tipping line from the tunnel at level five, are evident before the old mill. The old quarrymens' houses are in occupation alongside the old line to the quarry, many with their original slate roofs. Of the original locos *Margaret* (Edward Cropper's second and third wives were both named Margaret, and both related to the eminent Victorian parliamentarian and historian Thomas Babington Macaulay) is housed at Scolton Manor museum near Haverfordwest.

2. Foel Cwmcerwyn

At 1760 feet/536 metres Foel Cwmcerwyn, or Preseli Top as it is known locally, is Pembrokeshire's highest point. Trig point and Bronze Age cairns on the summit. Richard Fenton, one of Pembrokeshire's notable historians, came here in 1806 in a party, with fine ladies in crinoline, to excavate the cairns. The urn he found has not survived, but a drawing of it indicates it to have been well decorated, suggestive of continuing contact with Ireland. Good views to the south of Rosebush and Llys y Frân reservoirs, and the Gower peninsula – on good days Snowdonia, the Wicklow Hills in Ireland, and maybe Devon. There was a small slate quarry, Craig y Cwm, below the summit, but it's remoteness made it a short lived concern.

WALK DIRECTIONS [-] indicates history note

1. Starting from the Tafarn Sinc in Rosebush **[1]** turn left and left again along Rosebush's street, passing the Old Post Office on your left. Continue on past the old quarry workings to reach the gate giving entry to Pantmaenog Forest (planted in the 1950s).

2. Ignore the track left, but continue ahead to shortly leave the forestry route where it bears right, and go ahead on a signposted bridleway keeping the fence on your left – can be wet after rain.

3. The bridleway ends where the track rejoins from the right. Continue ahead, ignore a sharp turning to the left, but bear left at two successive forks to reach the top of the forest at a gate.

4. Turn right, keeping the forest and fence to your right. Where the fence turns to the right bear right also and continue to reach a gate giving access to open moorland – view of the trig point on Foel Cwmcerwyn [2] ahead. Continue on the discernible path leading to the summit.

5. From the summit head down on a well defined path which will take you to a metal gate by the corner of the forestry boundary fence. Continue downhill alongside the fence on the old track which once carried slate from Craig y Cwm quarry. Descend to meet a metal gate, go through, and continue ahead on the track, but this time with a fence on your left.

6. Part way down, where the forestry ends, there is metal gate on the right giving access to the forest – continue past this keeping an eye out for two stiles leading off the path to right and left.

7. When reached cross the waymarked stile on your right and cross fields, keeping the hedge on your left. Bear left onto a track which continues to Pant Mawr farm but almost immediately leave this track and going through a wooden gate enter a field and descend to meet the road through Rosebush. Bear left to return to the starting point.

FACILITIES

All available either in Rosebush or nearby Maenclochog. Pant Mawr Farmhouse Cheeses operate from Pant Fawr farm – it has it's own shop and website, and acts as the Post Office. The caravan park, for adults only, houses part of the old railway halt, lakes, and a memorial to Edward Cropper, the Hon Mrs Owen and JB Macaulay, erected by public subscription in 1913 in thanks for their efforts in constructing the Maenclochog Railway. No public access.

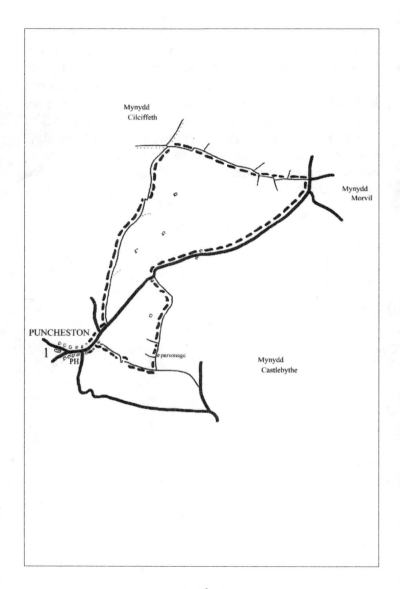

Mynydd
Cilciffeth

Mynydd
Morvil

PUNCHESTON
1
PH

parsonage

Mynydd
Castlebythe

6. puncheston

5.25 miles/8 kilometres

OS Maps: 1:25 000 North Pembrokeshire Outdoor Leisure 35.
Start: Drovers' Arms in Puncheston.
Access: Puncheston is easily reached from Letterston on the A40 Fishguard road, or from the Fishguard to Rosebush B4313 and from the B4329 Haverfordwest mountain road north to Cardigan. Buses 343 Fishguard to Haverfordwest stops Fridays only, 345 Mynachlog-ddu to Fishguard Thursdays only.
Parking: Plenty of parking space in the village.
Grade: Moderate.

The Drovers' Arms, Puncheston (01348 881469)
As it name suggests the pub traces it's origins back to the days of the drovers who used it as a meeting place. Travelling between farms and fairs and markets with cattle, sheep, pigs or geese the walk travels along part of their main drove route from Fishguard across the Preseli hills to Crymych – that section from Mynydd Cilciffeth to Mynydd Morvil. Dating back to at least the mid 19th century the pub was partly rebuilt after a fire in 1957, with modernisation and extension a few years later, and a new restaurant in 1973. Food is available. Open all day.

HISTORY NOTES
1. Puncheston (*Cas-mael*)

Puncheston takes it's name from Pontchardon in Normandy, France, which was the home of a Norman knight who settled here, and who gave his homeland's name to the area. The village's Welsh name, Cas-mael, may well derive from a stronghold built by a Welsh chief by name of Mael. Sited on the banks of the river Anghof that runs through the village it may have been built on by the later Norman knight, and whose simple castle would have been among a number built across the county to act as defence of the newly acquired territories. The site is still discernible, along the lane from Castle Green, which is passed through close to the end of the walk. It's church, overlooking the main road through the village, is dedicated to St Mary and dates from restoration in 1895, though it is known that there was a church here in the Middle Ages. It's two chapels, one Baptist, one Methodist, both from the 1820s, testify to the strong non conformist traditions from the 17th century onwards, both locally here and nationally; one local religious revival in 1795 was to become known as the Puncheston Revival. As well as places of worship they acted as cultural centres; one locally born poet winning the chair at the National Eisteddfod as well as at the Chicago International Eisteddfod in 1893. The Fishguard and North Pembrokeshire Railway arrived in the 1890s from nearby Rosebush and it's connections on to Carmarthenshire, linking Puncheston with Letterston and Fishguard. The railway was not a success and was soon bought out by the Great Western Railway;

however despite occasional closures services in one form or another stuttered on and off until final closure to goods traffic in 1949.

WALK DIRECTIONS [-] indicates history note

1. Starting from the Drovers' Arms in Puncheston [1] walk through the village, past the church, and where the road forks in two bear right, signposted for Maenclochog. After a short distance bear left onto a signposted bridleway. Continue uphill; for most of the route it is a broad track, becoming a path alongside fields where the track ends at a gate.

2. At the end of the path meet two bridleway gates set a little apart. Continue through the right hand one giving access to a field, bear right, and continue ahead with a fence to your right. Enter a larger field and this time continue with a bank and fence to your left. Continue on to gain access to fields leading down to the Maenclochog Fishguard road, this time keeping to the right.

Route down from Mynydd Cilciffeth

3. Once at the road bear right and right again, and follow the minor road downhill – signposted Puncheston. Ignore the road leading off left to Morvil. Continue downhill for over a mile / 1½ kilometres until after a sharp left hand bend leave the road and continue ahead on a track. Bridleway sign here, as well as a sign for Wern.

4. Continue on the track as it crosses the old railway line and follow it as it bears to the right through remains from the old Castlebythe slate quarry, in operation for much of the 19th and early 20th centuries. Where the track goes sharp left continue ahead across fields, keeping hedgebanks on your left, to meet the track giving access to Parsonage.

5. Continue ahead on the track until where the track bears left to the road, bear right and cross stiles to enter a rough field. Well signposted. Continue downhill keeping to the right edge to gain an attractive green lane. Follow this down until just before barns bear right into a field and then immediately left to shortly cross a footbridge, and bearing right go through gates and down steps to meet a track. Well waymarked.

6. Continue ahead on the track, crossing the river, and continuing uphill bear left on a waymarked path just before a house and metal gate to reach a small metal gate. Bear right, and passing a sign for Castle Green, reach the main road. Bear left to reach the starting point.

FACILITIES
Nearest Letterston and Fishguard.

7. pontfaen anò cwm gwaun

5.5 miles/8.75 kilometres

OS Maps: 1:25 000 North Pembrokeshire Outdoor Leisure 35.
Start: The Dyffryn Arms in Pontfaen.
Access: Pontfaen is on the minor road running through Cwm Gwaun – access from the B4313 from Fishguard, or from Dinas or Newport. Seasonal Cwm Gwaun Bus runs July to September, Tuesdays and Thursdays – contact Tourist Information Centres for details, or phone current contact number 0800 783 1584.
Parking: Parking at the side of the road opposite the Dyffryn.
Grade: Moderate.

The Dyffryn Arms, Pontfaen (01348 881305)
Long time Pembrokeshire favourite the Dyffryn Arms started life in 1845 as the Holly Bush – it's name (in Welsh *Llwyn Celyn*) and opening year were inscribed above the door. It's present name dates from the early 20th century, the pub having remained in the same family's hands since then. It's landlady, Bessie Davies, has become inseparable from the pub, and the Dyffryn is known locally as Bessie's. It's interior has remained largely unchanged since the last war, a welcome relief from some of the many recent experimentations on interior design. It has black and red floor tiles and a rough fireplace, possibly dating from the 1960s. Beer is dispensed into the glass from a jug, served through a

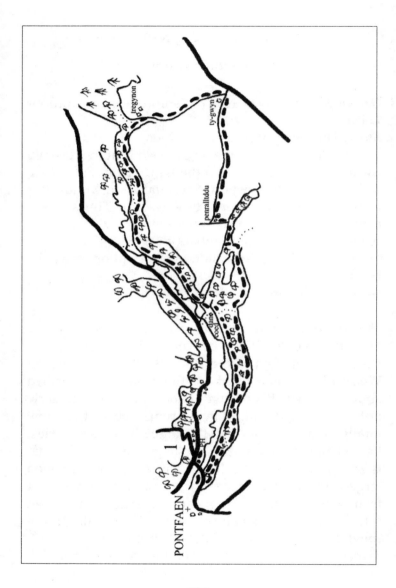

hatch opened for service, and closed afterwards. Entrance down a passageway to the right of the building. Beer garden to the right.

HISTORY NOTES
1. Pontfaen and Cwm Gwaun

The delightful Cwm Gwaun (*gwaun* is Welsh for moor) was formed as a sub glacial meltwater channel of the formidable Irish Sea glacier. Rising on the slopes of Foel Eryr in the Preseli hills the river Gwaun runs for 8½ miles / 14 kilometres down to Lower Fishguard, hence Fishguard's Welsh name of Abergwaun – mouth of the river Gwaun. It's slopes are densely wooded with oak, with alder and willow clinging close to the river. The Gwaun valley, along with the Daugleddau estuary and the National Nature Reserves of Tŷ Canol and Pengelli Forest near Felindre Farchog, is one of the few remaining areas of ancient woodland left in Pembrokeshire, and is an area of rare beauty, it's river meandering on it's course past small farms and the occasional isolated settlement. The dippers and grey wagtails that frequent the hidden rock pools and the river make a fine contrast with the wild moorland pipits, larks and buzzards. The valley's steep slopes have helped to keep communities and the natural landscape apart from the rest of the county, and preserve local traditions and individuality. When the new Gregorian calendar replaced the Julian calendar in 1752 local tradition ignored it. The Gwaun valley has the distinction of sharing with Lerwick in the Shetland Islands a New Year's Day of January 13th. The tradition of celebrating on January 13th persisted in the valley, many farmhouses hosting a party on *Hen Galan* (Old New Year's Day) with home brewed beer. Pontfaen (literally *Stone Bridge*) is typical of the small settlements that dot the valley. It's church, in ruins by 1861, was rescued from dereliction by the Arden family of Pontfaen House – it's nave and chancel probably date from circa 1200. There are 9th century memorial stones in the churchyard. The church is dedicated to the 6th century St Brynach, who lived for a while as a hermit on nearby Carn Ingli, the Rock of Angels.

Cwm Gwaun

WALK DIRECTIONS [-] indicates history note

1. Starting from the Dyffryn Arms in Pontfaen **[1]** walk the short distance to the crossroads and bear left uphill in the direction of the Maenclochog to Fishguard minor road. Continue past the small parking area on the left as this will be the end point of the walk to reach another path leading off left by a telegraph pole – there is a Public Footpath sign on the pole. Pontfaen's church,

signposted, is almost directly ahead on the right; worth a visit.

2. Continue ahead on the path through the wood, passing two paths leading off to the left, one fairly soon after entering the path, the other after approximately a mile / 1½ kilometres. Continue to reach a signposted choice of paths. Bear left over a footbridge and ascending steps reach a signposted bridleway. Bear right.

3. After a short distance the track breaks in two. Bear left to reach Penralltddu. Follow the waymarks past the barns and crossing the farmyard follow the track leading on to a minor road. Just before the minor road, at Ty-gwyn, bear left onto the track leading to Tregynon.

4. Once at Tregynon follow the waymarked path through the grounds, keeping the pond on your right. Ignore the path leading off to the right by the pond to continue ahead and left to re-enter the Gwaun valley woodland. Follow the path as it descends to meet a level path by a three way signpost. Bear left and continue ahead ignoring the turning to Sychbant en route to reach a track at Dan Coed.

5. Follow the route ahead over a footbridge and continue on the path as it ascends around the back of Dan Coed. Stay ahead, ignoring paths leading off to the left uphill, to reach the small parking area passed at the beginning of the walk. Bear right to return to the Dyffryn Arms.

FACILITIES

Continuing the tradition of brewing in the valley is the microbrewery of the Gwaun Valley Brewery – it's ales on sale in the county. Situated on the Maenclochog Fishguard road, visitors welcome. Penlan Uchaf gardens and café, on the road from Pontfaen through the valley in the direction of Newport, open early spring to late autumn. Sychbant picnic site and toilets on the left, just before Penlan Uchaf.

8. mynyðð ðinas anð aberfforest

8 miles/12.75 kilometres

Note: Can be combined with the 3 miles / 4.75 kilometres walk around Dinas Head at Walk 11 for a longer outing. Alternatively the walk could be split into two shorter ones, the Mynydd Dinas and Aberfforest sections.

OS Maps: 1:25 000 North Pembrokeshire Outdoor Leisure 35.
Start: The Ship Aground in Dinas Cross.
Access: Dinas Cross is on the A487 Fishguard to Newport and Cardigan road. The Ship Aground is on the left, just after turning off the A487 in the centre of the village, on the road to Bryn-henllan and Pwllgwaelod. Buses 405 The Poppit Rocket Cardigan to Fishguard daily May to September, and 412 Cardigan to Fishguard and Haverfordwest Monday to Saturday.
Parking: Parking in the village on the road down to Pwllgwaelod. Free car park if patronising the Ship Aground's car park – otherwise charge of £10!
Grade: Moderate.

Freemasons' Arms, Dinas Cross (01348 811243)
Dates back to at least the 1870s. Now occupying two adjacent properties the terrace in which it stands dates back to the 1830s. At one time it was a hotel, now self catering accommodation is available. Attractive and cosy interior with a large garden at the back, together with a

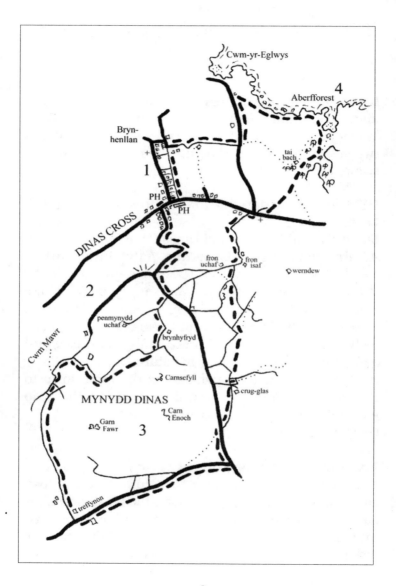

Cwm-yr-Eglwys

Aberfforest

4

Bryn-
henllan

1

PH

PH

DINAS CROSS

tai
bach

werndew

fron
uchaf

fron
isaf

2

penmynydd
uchaf

brynhyfryd

Cwm Mawr

Carnsefyll

MYNYDD DINAS

Carn
Enoch

Garn
Fawr

3

treffynon

patio area, with lots of flowers and lights. Dogs are welcome in the garden as long as on a lead. Open all day. Food available.

The Ship Aground, Dinas Cross (01348 811261)
An attractive pub with lots of memorabilia around it's walls, including paintings of ships and bright brass plates. Large fireplace for winter days. The origins of the pub are not certain, records referring not only to the pub but also to the village were kept in the church down in Cwm-yr-Eglwys, but these, along with the church, were destroyed in a great storm of the 1850s. It may date back to the mid 18th century, though it's earliest mention dates to 1851 when it may have been sited in a cottage and bakery opposite it's present site. The origin of it's name is also uncertain, however there are any number of Ship Inns, as well as Ships Aground or Afloat, in coastal towns and villages, and Dinas Cross has long been favoured by ships masters as a home. One late 19th century landlord spent his life at sea, his wife tending the inn. There have been a number of extensions over the years to meet it's continuing popularity. Food available. Outside seating. Open all day.

HISTORY NOTES
1. Dinas Cross
Locally normally referred to as just Dinas the origin of the name probably derives from an ancient fort once sited on Dinas Head, the Welsh *dinas* can be translated as fortress. It is a popular village with both locals and visitors. The village of Bryn-henllan (*old church hill*)

adjoins Dinas Cross, and as it's name suggests may have been the site of the original church before it was relocated down to Cwm-yr-Eglwys.

2. Viewpoint and Cwm Mawr

The viewpoint is sited on the old cliff's edge that, about a million years ago, would have marked the land's edge. Down below Dinas Cross and the land adjacent to the A road would have been under water, the harder volcanic rocks more resistant than the softer shales and mudstones below. Traces of sea stack and caves can still be found. Marked on the OS map Cwm Mawr (*big valley*) is a glacial meltwater channel cut out some 200,000 years ago across what was then a headland on the old coastline.

3. Mynydd Dinas

Mynydd Dinas

Part of Pembrokeshire's upland scenery Mynydd Dinas (*Dinas Mountain*), though on a smaller scale than the main Preseli hills, is still typical of the landscape pattern, with rock outcrops and the common land grazed by ponies and mountain sheep. The heather and gorse that cover the slopes are subject to spring burning, to provide good summer grazing. The main rocky outcrops of Garn Fawr, Carn Enoch and Carnsefyll are distinctive in that their grainy texture provides perhaps the best bouldering challenges in Pembrokeshire, several named routes offering climbing possibilities. The area has been covered by glacier ice at least twice in it's history. Great views from St David's peninsula in the west to Fishguard and Newport Bays, and the soft outlines of the Preseli hills.

4. Aberfforest

This is one of north Pembrokeshire's small intimate coves, with sand at low water. Popular with small boat owners and the occasional windsurfer. Few crowds here, and safe bathing. The pleasant wooded valley leading down to the beach does have one of Pembrokeshire's few waterfalls, with a small pool below it, though of no great depth.

WALK DIRECTIONS [-] indicates history note

1. In Dinas Cross [1] start from the Ship Aground, in Feidr Fawr (*big lane*), and head to the A road to turn right, and then shortly left into the residential street of Spring Hill. Signposted for Cwm Gwaun and Viewpoint. Follow the road as it wends it's way uphill to reach the viewpoint [2]. Convenient benches at the viewpoint.

2. The tarmac No Through Road leading ahead from the viewpoint would take you to the slopes of Mynydd Dinas, however continue ahead uphill on the B road to shortly

bear right onto the track leading to Penmynydd Uchaf. Signposted.

3. Where the main track bears right to Penmynydd Uchaf continue left until, just before a house ahead (Brynhyfryd), bear right onto a green lane to reach open fields and the slopes of Mynydd Dinas [3]. Bear right, not into the open field, but on a path alongside the stone wall.

4. Continue ahead across stiles and through bracken and gorse until where a stone wall again adjoins the path to form a right angled field corner bear right, and follow the path downhill with the wall to your right. Old lichened fingerpost here. There is, before the path turns to the right, another well defined path which leads off ahead and slightly left, but this eventually meets animal tracks leading across the slopes. It is possible to walk up to the rocks of Garn Fawr above, but there is no defined path. Once at the rocks you would need to cross the fence by them to gain the other side of Mynydd Dinas.

5. Continue downhill to the path's junction with a green lane. Right would take you to where the No Through Road from the viewpoint ends. Bear left and continue ahead. Ignore a path leading off downhill right and continue as the path wends its way ahead to meet a choice of paths at a field entrance. Bear left here, not ahead through the field entrance, and continue uphill with the wall on your right, to cross a stile and bear right. Signposted.

6. Continue on the path, keeping field boundaries to your right, to reach derelict buildings. Pass these on your right to gain the track giving access to Treffynon on your left. Continue to the road and bear left. Though not on

the route a short distance to the right, set into the hedge, are four standing stones and four fallen, marking out Parc y Meirw (*the field of the dead*), a probable Bronze Age alignment which would have been the longest in Wales. Marked as standing stones on the OS map.

7. Continue on the road to reach again the open slopes of Mynydd Dinas where fields end. Either continue ahead on the road to turn left at the junction, or cross the slopes to cut off the corner choosing your own route – no clear path here. There is a wide path leading off left across the slopes where the fields end, but this bears back left away from the route.

8. Just past a rough parking area on the left leave the road and follow a rough path adjacent to fields to reach the access road to Crug-glas. Cross the access road to reach a stile giving access to a small field on the right. Cross and bear left over another stile. The stile and route ahead would take you down to the main A road via Werndew, but it is a longer route.

9. Once in the field follow the line of the rough wall in the centre of the field until it comes close to a right angled field wall boundary on the left. Bear left just past here and go though a field gate to enter another field. Continue across the centre of the field on a path through the bracken – too close to the rocks on your left and you will have to step through the bracken. Continue to reach a stile in the field wall ahead.

10. Cross the stile and bear right and follow the path downhill and then around to the left to reach the track by Fron Uchaf. Bear right and passing Fron Isaf head down to meet the main A road.

11.   Cross, bear right, and then shortly left, down steps to cross a stile into a field. Signposted *To The Coast Path*. Keeping the hedge to your left continue to reach a stile. Cross and go over the stream on a stone footbridge and follow the path between fence and stream. Cross another footbridge to meet a T junction. Bear left and continue to reach the waterfall.

12.   Bear left, to pass in front of the waterfall, and continue on the path via stepping stones to emerge at Aberfforest **[4]**. If not descending to the waterfall pool it is possible to continue ahead and cross the lip of a dam and go up steps to emerge by a house. Bear right here onto a drive and just past the entrance to Aberfforest houses and Marine bear left, to again bear shortly left to Aberfforest.

Aberfforest

13.   From the beach cross the footbridge and continue on the Coast Path. The path inland would take you up

via Tai Bach to the road down to Cwm-yr-Eglwys. Where the Coast Path meets the road to Cwm-yr-Eglwys bear left, continue inland, to bear right opposite the turning to Tai Bach. Signposted.

14. Continue on the path and green lane, passing the caravan park on your left. Ignore a footpath signposted and leading off left en route by the caravan park, and continue on the bridleway to reach houses and tarmac road. Where the road turn sharp right by a domestic garage bear left onto a path and continue to reach the A road through Dinas Cross opposite the Freemasons' Arms. Bear right to regain the starting point.

FACILITIES

All available in Dinas Cross. Chip shop adjacent to the Freemasons' Arms.

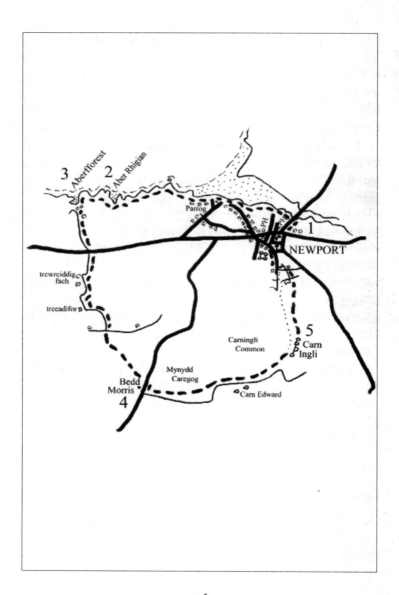

9. newport and carn ingli

9 miles/14.5 kilometres

OS Maps: 1:25 000 North Pembrokeshire Outdoor Leisure 35.
Start: The Golden Lion in Newport.
Access: Newport is on the A487 between Fishguard and Cardigan.
Parking: Limited parking in the Golden Lion car park opposite the inn for patrons, town car park in Long Street opposite the National Park Information Centre, and free down on the Parrog. Free parking by Newport bridge. Buses 405 The Poppit Rocket daily during summer May to September, less frequently during Winter; 412 Cardigan – Fishguard – Haverfordwest.
Grade: Strenuous.

Golden Lion Inn, East Street, Newport (01239 820321) www.goldenlionpembrokeshire.co.uk
A cosy and comfortable inn offering accommodation and food. Separate restaurant. Beer garden to side with picnic tables, with more set amongst shrubs to the rear, along with a patio and lawn further back. In it's late 18th century incarnation it was known as the Green Dragon, but the name was changed in 1830 to it's present one – it's then owners were the Bowen family of nearby Llwyngwair mansion, and whose coat of arms featured a golden lion. There is said to be a ghostly presence in the former servants quarters in the attic. The inn is dog friendly. Open all day.

The Castle Hotel, Bridge Street, Newport (01239 820742) www.castleinnnewport.co.uk

Built as the Commercial Inn in about 1876 by a Captain William Davies one early venture was the daily operation of a conveyance from the inn to the train station at Crymych. The only accident reported during it's twenty three years of operation was the death of a horse, due to old age, which fell in harness on the Cardigan road. With the retirement of Captain Davies in 1902 the coach service transferred to the Royal Oak. It's present name was adopted in 1960. Accommodation and food available. Dogs welcome. Open all day.

The Royal Oak, West Street, Newport (01239 820632)

Originally the Butchers' Arms the pub would seem to have been in operation for most of the 19th century, with a short period of closure mid century. On it's reopening the name was changed to the Royal Oak. Since the late 1990s there has been an emphasis on food, and it's restaurant has been enlarged. Specialises in grills and curries. Open all day. There is a car park at the rear for patrons.

HISTORY NOTES

1. Newport

The earliest man made structure remaining in the Newport town area is the Neolithic burial chamber of Carreg Coetan Arthur. Dated to 3500BC excavations in 1979 and 1980 showed that it had been surrounded and partially covered by a circular cairn of subsoil. Ploughing has built up a high level of soil around the uprights; the original structure would have originally appeared much taller. It's capstone now rests on two of it's original four sidestones. One of a number of such structures within the Newport and Nevern area it would have served the original farming community here who would have made a living through crop cultivation and animal husbandry, as well as river and coastal fishing, the river Nyfer which has it's outlet at Newport is still noted for it's salmon and trout. It's present name is one of many early structures to be associated with Arthur; in this case he used the stones (*carreg*) of the chamber to play *coetan* or quoits. Finds at the site include an axe fragment, flint knives and scrapers, and pottery fragments from probable cremation urns as charcoal and pieces of cremated human bone were found with them. It is in comparatively good condition and is signposted and easily found amongst modern bungalows on the left of Feidr Pen-y-Bont, the road leading down to Newport's late 19th century bridge across the Nyfer.

Settlement continued through the Iron Age and the early medieval period, but Newport's development as a town had to wait until the building of it's castle by the Norman William fitz Martin who had been driven out of his castle at Nevern by his father in law, the Lord Rhys, in 1191. The town that grew up in it's shadow was incorporated and given the name of *Novus Burgus*, New Town, or port. Fitz Martin also established St Mary's church, possibly on the site of an earlier 7th century church to St Curig. The castle was captured by the Welsh in 1215 and again in 1257, and may have been damaged in 1405 during the revolt of Owain Glyndŵr. By the 16th century it was in ruins, remaining so until the gatehouse and a flanking tower were converted into a private residence in 1859. It remains in private hands. The 13th century church retains it's original cruciform plan, but little of it's original structure remains apart from the 13th century stepped buttressed three storied tower. The church was enlarged in 1835, and then rebuilt in 1854, only to be restored in 1879. It's roof has been replaced. There is a fine Norman font, and close to it, set into the wall, a medieval holy water stoup. There is in the vestry a 14th century floriated cross-slab.

Newport became the capital of the Norman lordship of Cemais and received privileges from William fitz Martin – the right to the annual appointment of mayor of Newport, with jurisdiction over a Court Leet, still exists. Despite a dangerous sand bar across the river mouth which hindered harbour development Newport had by the 16th century come to rival Fishguard in coastal trade. Out went slate to local ports and to Ireland, and slate stones to Bristol; herrings to France and Spain. For a while in the mid 16th century it was a woolen manufacturing centre with trade links with Bristol, which were to decline with an outbreak of plague, and a loss of trade to Fishguard. Alongside coastal trade and fishing went shipbuilding, and the town had a thriving shipyard by the end of the 18th century. The Parrog shipyards became noted; before 1830 for it's square rigged ships, after for it's schooners. In 1825 a new quay was built, trade increased, and the area, with it's shipyards, storehouses and coal yards became a bustle of activity. For a while, from 1800 to the 1830s, Newport was third only to Milford and Lawrenny in the number of sailing vessels built and registered at the local ports of Milford, Pembroke and Cardigan. In came coal from Cardiff, slate from Gloucester, bricks from Cardigan, but with the development of land links the coastal trade inevitably declined, and the last vessel to call, the *Agnes*, landed her cargo of coal in September 1934. The quay walls survive, though in poor condition, and the last of the storehouses has become the Newport Boat Club. There is a double limekiln in good condition, with next to it the old limeburner's cottage. There is a slipway for launching dinghies, and dinghy sailing has become a popular sport here.

Newport has north Pembrokeshire's largest and most popular beach – Newport's Welsh name is after all *Trefdraeth*, which can be translated as Beach Town. Lots of firm sand it is really two beaches, the larger and more popular Traethmawr (*big beach*) on the north side of the

Newport Bay and Newport from Carn Ingli

river, and the smaller Parrog Sands by the old harbour. It is possible to wade across the river at low tides. Traethmawr is backed by sand dunes, with parking allowed, at present, on the beach itself – there is also a car park. The estuary of the river Nyfer offers a variety of habitats to local and visiting bird populations. As well as the trees alongside the river there are the mudflats, salt and freshwater marsh, and reed beds. As well as any number of mallard and gulls, recent visitors have included the little egret, often seen fishing to the right of the bridge by the reed bed, and a great number of geese. Needless to say the river and the area around the bridge are popular spots for local birdwatchers.

2. Aber Rhigian

One of Pembrokeshire's many small indented bays Aber Rhigian is backed by woodland, and close to and visible from the main A road to Newport, the unique circular 4th to early 3rd millennium BC Neolithic burial chamber of Cerrig y Gof (*Rock of the Smith*). Shingle and pebble backed the bay has sand at low tides.

3. Aberfforest

Like Aber Rhigian another small unspoilt bay. Sandy at low tides, and popular with dinghy sailors. The limekiln at the head of the beach would have been in use in the days when local limestone, usually brought in direct by boat to beach, was burnt to provide lime for Pembrokeshire's acid soils.

4. Bedd Morris

The standing stone here traditionally marks the grave of Morris, or Morus, hence the Welsh name Bedd (*grave*) Morris. Morris himself was a notorious highwayman who took shelter amongst the rocks commanding the road down to Newport. Preferring bow and arrow as his method of attack, he trained his dog to retrieve any arrows that failed to meet their target. Incensed at his behaviour Morris was taken by the local populace, hanged, and buried beneath the stone. The stone itself is probably Bronze Age in origin, and would no doubt have indicated an important trade route. It has served for centuries as a boundary stone to Newport parish, and *Newport* can still be picked out, cut into the stone.

5. Carn Ingli

Once the core of a volcano the views from the present summit of Carn Ingli are quite superb. To the north are the rocks of Snowdonia, with the full panorama of the Preseli hills swinging around you to your right, whilst the splendid sea coast of Newport and Fishguard Bays lie etched below. One theory suggests that Carn Ingli was enclosed in the Neolithic period, another that the hillfort here was built by Iron Age settlers; either way the fort is spectacular. The still impressive single defensive wall in it's heyday may have been ten feet/three metres high. Traceable in the landscape are numerous hut circles and enclosures. Possibly occupied until late Roman times it could have been home to some one hundred and fifty people. One notable Carn Ingli resident is said to have been the 6th century Irish St Brynach. A friend and contemporary of St David he founded a number of churches in the area, of which the church at Nevern, dating from 570, was the most important. Preferring to live the life of a hermit he chose Carn Ingli's splendid isolation as home. However St Brynach was no ordinary hermit. Not only was his coach driven by stags and his cows herded by a wolf, but he was also ministered to by a flight of angels. Quite possibly Carn Ingli takes it's name from the legend of St Brynach's life, and the Rock or Mount of Angels, Carn Engylion. In recent times stone was quarried from Carn Ingli's steep rock face and transported via a cable railway to a crushing plant on the road below to the east. Two stone pillar blocks at the head of the incline are all that now remain of this brief industrial intrusion. Carningli Common and Mynydd Caregog are typical of Pembrokeshire's upland scenery; gorse, bilberry and heather predominate, with on lower slopes occasional blocks of pine plantation. In late summer and autumn the yellows and purples of the gorse and heather turn the landscape into a glorious exhibition of colour.

WALK DIRECTIONS [-] indicates history note

1. Starting from the Golden Lion in Newport [1] walk up the main A road in the direction of Cardigan to shortly bear left onto Feidr Pen-y-Bont (*Pen-y-Bont lane*), the road leading to Newport's golf course and Traethmawr beach, and to Moylegrove. Passing Carreg Coeten Arthur burial chamber on the left (signposted), continue down to Newport's bridge.

2. Just before the bridge bear left onto a path leading alongside the river and follow it to meet the Parrog Road. Just after leaving the bridge, by tennis courts on the left, is the site of Yr Hen Castell. Marked as Enclosure on the OS map this may be a possible Iron Age fort or defensive harbour; alternatively it may be a

motte and bailey earthwork. It is known that William fitz Martin's castle was rebuilt on it's present site following destruction. Once at the Parrog Road bear right and follow the route of the Coast Path, either along the foreshore, or if necessary follow the high tide alternative – route clearly marked; route goes up steps on the right just after Rock House's drive.

3. Continue on the Coast Path to the sheltered and pretty coves of Aber Rhigian [2] and Aberfforest [3]. From Aberfforest, just before reaching the beach, take the path leading off left by steps and leading away from the coast to reach the road leading to Aberfforest houses and Marine, situated on the right. Follow the road left to reach the main A487.

4. Cross and bear right, and almost immediately bear left onto a marked bridleway. Currently there is a large sign for Havard Stables here. Continue inland, bearing left at Trewreiddig Fach and following the bridleway again shortly bear left and continue on the track to reach Trecadifor.

5. Pass the building on your right and follow a path uphill and where a choice of two paths are met bear left and follow an attractive green lane alongside a fence. Continue to reach a crossroads of paths. Continue uphill ahead and enter a field. Follow a clearly defined path through gorse and stay on it as it bears around to the left to emerge at a minor road. Bear right to reach the standing stone of Bedd Morris [4] and a small parking area on your left.

6. Just to the left of the parking area is a clearly defined path leading out across Mynydd Caregog. Stay on this

path, as it skirts fences to your right, and passing the rocks of Carn Edward en route finally reach Carn Ingli [5].

7. Choice to scramble up Carn Ingli's slopes and follow the path across the top through rocks, heather and bilberry, or stay on the flat and continue on a well defined path as it descends to fields. On meeting a field gate this route continues ahead, shortly bearing left, and at a concrete trackway it bears right, continuing downhill on a tarmac road, and passing the property of Castle Hill on the left.

8. If following the route across Carn Ingli descend and follow a clearly defined path down (this path is to the right of the flat path in front of Carn Ingli!) and where walled fields adjoin to the left and open country ends meet a fence and a gated track by a house on the right. Go through the gate and continue down, and at a crossroads of paths bear first left, and passing Bryn Eithin on your right meet a tarmac road. Castle Hill is on this road, uphill to the left. Bear right and continue downhill.

Carn Ingli pony

9. With both downhill routes meeting by Castle Hill simply descend. At College Square continue ahead and

by St Mary's church either bear right and left, or continue ahead to reach Market Street, and then down, to reach the main A road through Newport. Bear right to regain the starting point.

FACILITIES

All available in Newport. Public toilets on the Parrog. Golf course across the river. Newport is home to the Eco Centre Wales. Tourist Information Centre in Long Street, opposite the car park; toilets at the car park.

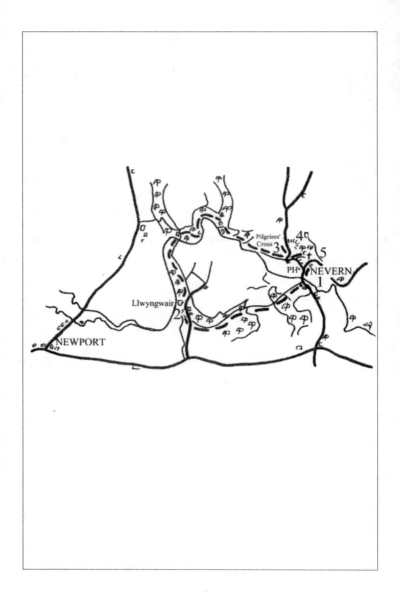

Pilgrims'
Cross

NEWPORT

Llwyngwair

NEVERN

PH

128

10. NEVERN

2.5 miles/4 kilometres

OS Maps: 1:25 000 North Pembrokeshire Outdoor Leisure 35.

Start: Trewern Arms in Nevern.

Access: Nevern is on the B4582, close to Newport, and a short distance from the A487 Newport to Cardigan road. Bus 412 Fishguard to Cardigan passes the turn to Nevern – the village is ½ mile / ¾ kilometre from here.

Parking: Car park at the Trewern Arms for patrons; limited parking also in the village.

Grade: Easy.

Trewern Arms (01239 820395)
This inn dates back to the 16th century, and is set in it's own grounds overlooking the tranquil river Nyfer. At one time the Bridgend Inn it acquired it's present name following sale in the 1850s. With it's acquisition in 1957 by Wing Commander Nelson-Edwards and his wife (a former Windmill Girl) the inn nearly doubled in size and became a popular pub restaurant. Now a hotel it still retains it's public bar, the *Brew House*, decorated with a great assortment of agricultural memorabilia and other bric a brac, with traditional settles set on it's original flagstone floor. Food and accommodation available in comfortable surroundings. Attractive garden, with lots of trees and shrubs.

HISTORY NOTES

1. Nevern

One of the prettiest villages in Wales Nevern has had a rich and colourful history, it's layout following the pattern of Norman settlement. It's river, rising to the east of Crymych in the north east of the county, is noted for it's fishing; sea and brown trout, and salmon. It's attractive bridge dates from the early 19th century. Nevern's old Welsh name is Nanhyfer, derived from an earlier Nant Nyfer, *nant* being the Welsh for brook.

2. Llwyngwair Manor

Llwyngwair Manor, now a hotel and caravan park, has a fine manor house. The country seat of the Bowens from 1540 until the family line recently died out the house has been much altered over the years, and is in effect an amalgam of styles from Tudor to Victorian. The Bowens were great patrons of the Methodists, John Wesley visited here, and William Williams Pantycelyn reputedly wrote what was to become one of the most popular of Welsh hymns here – possibly viewing Carn Ingli in one of it's bad moods he wrote *oe'r those gloomy hills of darkness, look my soul* ... Reflecting it's setting Llwyngwair translates as *hay grove*. Pontnewydd, *new bridge*, was built by the Bowens at a suitable crossing over the river Nyfer.

3. Pilgrims' Cross

Cut into the rock face here is the two foot high Pilgrims' Cross, with, below, a natural ledge where pilgrims may have knelt to supplicate the saints. Tradition has credited Nevern with being the last stage on the pilgrim route to St David's from St Dogmael's Abbey and North

Start of Nevern route

Wales. Certainly there were at one time eight pilgrim chapels of ease in Nevern parish, although by Elizabethan times they were in ruins. It is possible that this was the site of a healing well, Pistyll Brynach. Holy wells, springs, standing stones and Celtic church sites were much in favour as sources of bodily and/or spiritual strength. To the left of the cross, away from the road, are curious steps in the rock where the path begins a short ascent. No doubt cut by water there is a small graffiti cross cut into the stone. It is unlikely that pilgrims would have continued on the path to Newport, there are more direct routes, but pilgrimages were protracted affairs, with many side trips to different sites, and this would have been a wayside shrine, now almost unique.

4. Nevern castle

More properly called Castell Nanhyfer, Nanhyfer being the original name for Nevern, the site has been subject to recent excavations. It is a fine example of a motte and bailey castle. One find dating from the 2008 excavation was a 12th century Nine Men's Morris board and counter. It was Robert fitz Martin, a Norman landowner from Devon, who took the old hundred of Cemais for himself to create a Norman enclave within Welsh territory, who built a double-motted castle here circa 1108, on the site of an earlier Welsh stronghold and probably an Iron Age settlement. His son William fitz Martin, who inherited the castle, had married Angharad, the daughter of the Lord Rhys, the native ruler of Deheubarth (south-west Wales), however this did not prevent his father in law from driving him out in 1191, giving the castle to his son Maelgwyn. Maelgwyn, together with a brother, later repaid his father by imprisoning him at Nevern for a brief time. William fitz Martin re-established Norman influence in the area in 1204, building himself a more substantial castle at Newport, with it's easy access to the sea. Nevern castle would then seem to have been abandoned by both Welsh and Norman.

5. Nevern church

St Brynach, to whom the present church is dedicated, established a religious settlement in the 6th century. A native of Ireland he had made his way here after pilgrimage to Rome, followed by sojourn in Brittany. He established a number of churches in the area, but seems to have preferred to live the life of a hermit on Cārn Ingli, the *Rock of Angels*. A friend and contemporary of St David he is believed to have died on 7th April 570, St Brynach's day. Before they were driven out of Nevern the Normans had time to build a church on St Brynach's site, yet all that now remains is the 12th century tower. The rest of the church is late 14th century/early 15th century, and was much restored in 1864. The church and churchyard still, however, hold hidden treasure.

Embedded in the window sills of the south chapel, the Trewern-Henllys chapel, are two rare stone slabs found in 1906. The Maglocunus stone is a late 5th century or early 6th century memorial stone to *Maglocunus*, son *(fili) of Clutorius*. The inscriptions are in both Latin and ogham. Ogham is a script developed in Ireland by the late 5th century and is made up of a series of lines cut across the edge of the stone. Each letter of this Latin based alphabet is named from a tree or plant eg b from beith (birch). Next to it is the fine 10th century Cross Stone, with it's interlaced two cord cross. There is another bilingual

Nevern cross

memorial stone outside by the porch, to the 5th/6th century Welsh chieftain Vitalianus. However the pride of Nevern is the magnificent late 10th or early 11th century Great Cross – there are other superb examples at Carew and Penally in the south of the county. Inscribed on both sides only the meaning of that on the back of the cross can be guessed at – the letters DNS an abbreviation of the Latin *Dominus*, Lord. In former days the first cuckoo of

Spring is said to have sung from the head of the stone on St Brynach's day.

The fine avenue of English yews is believed to be six hundred years old – the second yew on the right from the churchyard entrance is famous for the almost continuous blood red sap that drips, some say, for a monk who was wrongly hung from the branches above. The line of Irish yews along the road were planted as a memorial to those who fought in the First World War. The mounting block by the entrance is one of only two left in Pembrokeshire, no doubt the occasional horse rider still makes use of it. The Nevern valley features in the medieval tales of the Mabinogion, for Twrch Trwyth, the wild boar, was pursued through the valley by Arthur and his knights to the Preseli hills. Nowadays the river is hunted only for salmon and sewin, returning from the sea at Newport Bay.

WALK DIRECTIONS [-] indicates history note

1. Starting in Nevern [1] take the footpath leading across the field between the Trewern Arms and Nevern bridge – access next to a metal field gate. Signposted with walking man symbol. Cross the field to a wooded green lane and continue to reach the minor road by Llwyngwair Manor (now a hotel and caravan park) [2] – great views left en route of Carn Ingli's rock peak.

2. Bear right and continue past the old farm buildings. Where the road continues right to Llwyngwair Home farm continue ahead on a track, the route signposted just before a sign for Pontnewydd on the right. Continue to reach a footpath leading right, just past the bridge and

the house on the left. Continue on this path, past a ruined cottage, to gain the riverside path.

3. Where the path meets a concrete roadway by a private house continue straight ahead across a footbridge, cross another private roadway and again go straight ahead to turn immediately right, waymarked. Cross the centre of the field to a stile to reach a path high above the river. Continue on this to reach another field.

4. Go ahead across the field, and keeping to the right field edge, reach a stile at the top right of the field. Cross onto the path leading past the Pilgrims' Cross [3] to reach the road into Nevern.

5. At the road bear left uphill to the main castle site [4] entrance – field gate here. Either return back down this road, passing the access to the Pilgrims' Cross, or take the footpath leading downhill from the bailey, the cleared area in front of the old motte on which the old timber or stone tower would have stood – the path is not that easy to find but it is just past the ditch in front of the tower, descending through trees. If taking the road route where the road bears right continue ahead on a footpath by the side of a house to reach Nevern church [5] across an attractive stone footbridge. The route from the castle site leads down to this access path, just before the footbridge.

6. At the church continue along the footpath by the side of the church wall by a stream. From the church it is a short distance back to the starting point.

FACILITIES

BT telephone, public toilets (by the community hall).

Accommodation available in the village. Llwyngwair Manor is a popular caravan park. Pentre Ifan, possibly the finest Neolithic burial chamber in Britain, is two miles / three and a quarter kilometres to the south on a minor road; Castell Henllys, a recreation of an Iron Age fort, is two miles / three and a quarter kilometres to the north on the A487. Both are signposted.

11. Dinas Head

3 miles/4.75 kilometres

Note: Dinas Head often gets referred to as Dinas island, owing more to it's geologiocal history than it's present geography. Combine with Walk 8 for a much longer walk.

OS Maps: 1:25 000 North Pembrokeshire Outdoor Leisure 35.
Start: Pwllgwaelod.
Access: Pwllgwaelod is reached from the village of Dinas Cross, on the A487 Fishguard to Newport road. Bus 405 Fishguard to Cardigan (the Poppit Rocket) calls at Pwllgwaelod daily during it's summer timetable May to September, bus 412 Haverfordwest to Fishguard to Cardigan calls at Dinas Cross all year round.
Parking: Free parking at Pwllgwaelod. Parking also possible at Cwm-yr-Eglwys.
Grade: Moderate.

The Old Sailors, Pwllgwaelod (01348 811491)
Re-opened in 2006 after closing in the mid 1990s there has been a notable pub here in one form or another over the last hundred and thirty years or so. Originally named the Sailor's Safety one tradition has it that is was so named because a light was displayed after dark to guide sailors (and smugglers) across Fishguard Bay to the safety of the shore; more prosaically it was a simple indication of safety or rest, it's first recorded landlord

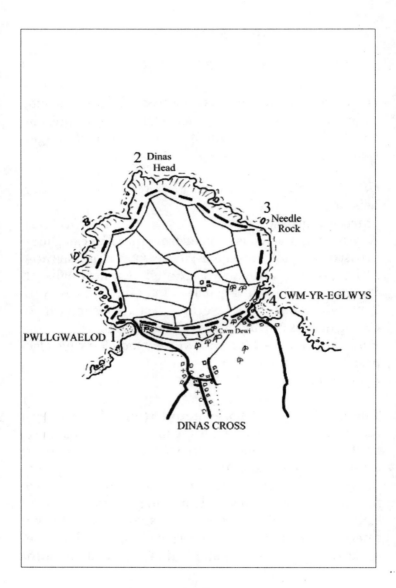

2 Dinas Head

3 Needle Rock

CWM-YR-EGLWYS 4

PWLLGWAELOD 1

5 Cwm Dewi

DINAS CROSS

from 1867 to the early 1880s was a master mariner. Tradition has also dated it's origins, without recorded proof, to 1593. The original Sailor's Safety occupied what is now a private residence adjacent to the present building – it's focus as a pub was shifted when in the mid 1940s the then landlord built a new building adjacent to it which became the new pub; it had a high roof to help disperse cigarette smoke and an imported former carved wooden ship's dresser from Kolkata, India, which became the bar. The bar is no more, the present Sailor's now occupies the refurbished Sailor's Safety and the old adjacent café. The bay is popular with local fishermen; locally caught fish often find their way onto the restaurant and bar's menu. The garden area fronts onto the beach, and has great views over the bay. Currently open all days 11.00 to 18.00 except Mondays, open from 19.00 on Fridays and Saturdays for meals. Dogs welcome.

HISTORY NOTES
1. Pwllgwaelod
Pwllgwaelod, which can be translated as bottom pool, has always been popular, and can get crowded on hot summer days. Still popular with local fishermen the small car park at the head of the beach often doubles up as a boat park. The limekiln, a little way inland from the beach, would have produced lime for fertilising Dinas Island farm, and farms around Dinas Cross.
2. Dinas Head
Dinas Head, or rather Pen y Fan (*head of the peak*), stands at 466 feet/142 metres high. It's survival as a

Dinas Head and Dinas Cross

headland is due to the Silurian grits of which it is partly formed, harder rock than the surrounding softer Ordovician shales and sandstones which have fallen victim to the sea's adventuring. There are the ruins of a former coastguard lookout by the OS trig point. In addition to Newport Bay there are magnificent views south over Fishguard Bay to Garn Fawr and Strumble Head, and inland to Dinas Cross and the outlying hills of the Preseli range. From the headland there are good chances of seeing seals in the waters below, perhaps even a harbour porpoise or dolphin. Local tales tell of a fisherman who when he cast anchor off the headland received an unexpected visitor. One of the fairy folk, the Bendith y Mamau, who had their city under the sea here, climbed up the anchor rope and complained the anchor had gone through his roof. Dinas Island farm, some four hundred acres, was once an Elizabethan grange which provided game for the formerly splendid Pentre Ifan mansion, near Newport. Former holders have included the naturalist Ronald Lockley, founder of Britain's first bird observatory at Skokholm, who raised cattle, sheep, corn and early potatoes for a number of years and wrote of his time there in *Island Farmer* and *Golden Year*.

3. Needle Rock

The attraction here is Needle Rock, the great sea stack which provides a grand home for breeding guillemots and razorbills from April to July. With the clamour of breeding kittiwakes and gulls, jackdaws and fulmars this can be a noisy and entertaining place. There are usually a few young fulmars, hatched on the cliffs below, present until September, but most sea birds have by then left to overwinter at sea. Great views from here of Newport Bay, with Cardigan island and the great rock folds of Cemaes Head and Pen yr Afr in sight on clear days, with inland Carn Ingli and Newport, the castle and church tower just visible.

4. Cwm-yr-Eglwys

Cwm-yr-Eglwys (*valley of the church*), like it's close neighbour Pwllgwaelod, is one of the most popular beaches on the north coast, but unlike Pwllgwaelod with it's grey sand, has fine golden sand at low water. The 15th century church, of which only the western wall and belfry survive, was destroyed, along with low lying cottages and the quay, in a truly ferocious storm in October 1859 which wrecked shipping all around the Welsh coast. Of the 114 ships wrecked the worst was the

Royal Charter, sunk off Anglesey with the loss of 459 lives. A new church was built on safer ground, inland at Bryn-henllan, in 1860. Like it's predecessor it was dedicated to the 6th century St Brynach. One of the many coastal trading ports Cwm-yr-Eglwys was, at least in the late 18th century, known as Dinas Harbour. Sheltered as it is from the prevailing westerlies, the cove shows a marked difference in appearance to Pwllgwaelod. Trees and shrubs flourish here, adding their softer greens to the blues and greys of the sea and sky.

5. Cwm Dewi

Cwm Dewi is a pleasant marshy and wooded valley, popular with the local bird life, and watched over by the Dinas island rabbits and sheep. It was formed some 17,000 to 20,000 years ago as a meltwater channel for the glacier then blocking Newport Bay, making Dinas island truly an island. Later infills of boulder clay have helped form the valley as it is today.

WALK DIRECTIONS [-] indicates history note

1. Starting from Pwllgwaelod [1] head up the road to the left of the pub, and bearing left join the coast path to reach Dinas Head [2] – don't follow the road inland to the farm!

2. A short distance after leaving the headland there is a choice of paths. The coastal route drops down off the ridge, giving a better view of Needle Rock [3], though in wet weather or after rain it can be muddy. The drier route continues along the ridge. Both routes join by Cwm-yr-Eglwys [4].

3. Once at Cwm-yr-Eglwys, keeping initially to the right of the car park, follow the valley path along Cwm Dewi [5] the 0.5 miles / 0.75 kilometres back to Pwllgwaelod.

FACILITIES
Pwllgwaelod has public toilets, as does Cwm-yr-Eglwys. Most other facilities are available in Dinas Cross, including garage and mini market and two more pubs!

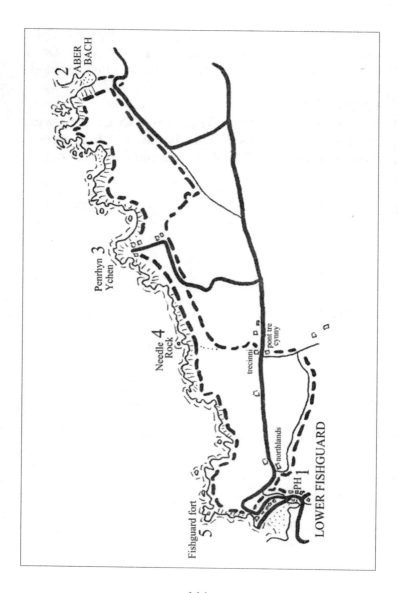

ABER BACH 2

Penrhyn Ychen 3

Needle Rock 4

pont tre cymmy

trecinni

northlands

Fishguard fort 5

LOWER FISHGUARD

PH 1

12. lower fishguard

7 miles/11 kilometres

OS Maps: 1:25 000 North Pembrokeshire Outdoor Leisure 35.
Start: Lower Fishguard.
Access: Marked as Lower Town on the OS map it is situated on the A487 main road to Cardigan. Bus routes 405 (the Poppit Rocket) Cardigan to Fishguard (May to Sept only) and 412 from Cardigan to Haverfordwest all year round. Other major bus routes connect with Fishguard town. Ferry from Ireland connects with Goodwick, with onward rail link.
Parking: Parking at Lower Fishguard harbour; the minor road to the harbour leads off from the main road and is signposted. There is no parking by the Ship Inn, as it fronts directly onto the road.
Grade: Moderate.

The Ship Inn, Lower Fishguard (01348 874033)
Situated on the narrow main road just before the road forks to the harbour and to Dinas Cross the inn forms part of the row of terraced houses just after the narrow bridge over the river Gwaun. There has been an inn here at least since 1817, maybe even from the late 1700s. It may have closed briefly during the mid 19th century, only to re-open in the late 1860s; possibly then adding the cottage bakery which stood next door to form it's present size. It successfully fought a hard battle in 1919 against the temperance movement who wanted it closed

because, according to their reasoning, it was not required. It remains, and has a homely feel, with an open fire for the colder months. Lots of seafaring and film memorabilia; both *Under Milk Wood* and *Moby Dick* were filmed in the area, Richard Burton, Elizabeth Taylor and Peter O'Toole intoning the words of Dylan Thomas in inimitable fashion, while Gregory Peck dreamt of the great white whale. Free house. Open all day.

HISTORY NOTES
1. Lower Fishguard
The Welsh name for Fishguard, Abergwaun, translates as mouth of the river Gwaun, the river that flows out into Lower Fishguard harbour. For similar reasons the lower town locally is also known as Cwm (the Welsh for valley). The Gwaun valley, with it's soft woodlands, is the most impressive meltwater channel in Britain, it's drowned western end forming the harbour. The name Fishguard may derive from *fiskrgard*, Scandinavian for a fish weir, however known use of it can only be dated back to the 13th century rather than back to Scandinavian influences on the coast, and there are in Goodwick the remains of two medieval fish traps built out from the sides of the bay, and this may be the origin. An important herring fishing port during the Elizabethan age it grew during the 18th century to be exceeded only by Haverfordwest in the volume of trade. Population grew, with exports of cured herrings, pilchards, corn, butter and slate, imports of coal, limestone, fabrics and food. By the late 18th century

Lower Fishguard

some fifty vessels were based here, with it's shipyard reaching it's best years in the second decade of the 19th. The pier and quay were built by local shipowner and merchant Samuel Fenton during the late 18th century; he also introduced a method of curing pilchards, exports of which went to the Mediterranean and the Baltic. However by the late 19th century trade and fishing had declined, and the shoals have moved on. Now mainly pleasure vessels dot the picturesque harbour.

2. Aber Bach

Sometimes also known as Aber Hescwm this secluded and attractive cove gets few visitors. Shingle and rock backed at high water, there is a little sand at low tides.

Pleasant spot for swimming, away from the crowds. Beach access also possible on the footpath through Hescwm mill from the road.

3. Penrhyn Ychen (*promontory of the oxen*)

There are the remains of a First World War lookout here, access down steps from the headland. Good views of the bay and the rocky beaches either side. Made of local Goodwick bricks, and so marked, the construction serves as a reminder of the many small brickwork companies which once operated in the county – Goodwick brickworks closed relatively recently in 1969.

4. Needle Rock

The rock is a superb isolated stack with an knife edged arch cut through it's base. The stack and adjacent cliffs provide nesting sites for fulmars, guillemots, razorbills, cormorants and gulls. Best viewed from the Coast Path on leaving the caravan park, close by it is difficult to see it at it's best, tucked as it is adjacent to the cliff.

5. Fishguard fort

The fort here dates from 1781, built as a defence against privateers. It has double ramparts and has four cannon, one from 1785 – originally it had eight 9-pounder guns and was manned by three invalid Woolwich gunners. The site gives a superb view of the harbour and would have provided a vantage point to the events of 1779 in response to which the fort had been constructed. In September of that year the *Black Prince*, a privateer crewed by English and Irish smugglers, had taken captive a local merchant ship owned by Samuel Fenton, and had demanded a ransom for it of £500, plus another £500 for the town. On being refused the cutter bombarded Fishguard, damaging chimneys and the roof of St Mary's church, as well as permanently injuring Mary Fenton, niece of Samuel Fenton. Fired on in reply by the Master of an armed smuggler then in port the *Black Prince* was forced to leave empty handed. With the end of the Napoleonic wars in 1815 the fort fell into disrepair.

WALK DIRECTIONS [-] indicates history note

1. Starting from the car park in the harbour join the main road through town **[1]**, and turn left onto it – the Ship Inn is to the right, on the far side of the road. Continue for a short distance uphill to bear right onto a No Through Road opposite a parking bay. Continue uphill to reach the main A road by metal posts and fence.
2. Almost immediately leave the main road, turning right at *Northlands*, to join a track. Signpost for bridleway on adjacent Telegraph pole. The track shortly becomes a green lane. Continue on the green lane to finally emerge into a field by farm buildings. Keep to the right hand side of the field, along and by a slight ridge, to reach a bridleway gate giving access to a farm track.
3. Turn left and continue to reach the main road by *Pont Tre Cynny*. Cross the road to reach a stile adjacent to *Trecinni*, on the building's right side. Bear diagonally right across the field to reach a track by a house. Bear left. Shortly great views open up of Fishguard Bay. Where the track goes downhill bear right onto a waymarked path.
4. After a short distance the path reaches a gate; continue on the path to reach a choice of signposted

routes; left is a permissive path leading down to Needle Rock and the Coast Path. Continue instead ahead uphill to shortly cross a stone wall stile. Crossing country reach the minor road leading to Fishguard Bay Caravan Park at a kissing gate.

5. Bear left and continue ahead, and where the road bears sharp left to the caravan park, by buildings, bear right onto a waymarked green lane going uphill. Signposted here for bridleway and *Ty Gwyneth*. Continue on this lane to reach a T junction of paths, well signposted. Bear left, and where a track is joined continue ahead. This track soon meets tarmac road leading down to Aber Bach – go ahead.

6. Continue down to Aber Bach **[2]**, access to the beach through a gated path leading off from the road where it bears sharp right. From Aber Bach retrace your steps back to the road and bear right uphill back the way you came. After the hairpin turn there are steps to the right giving access to the Coast Path; well signposted.

7. Continue on the Coast Path to reach the caravan park and Penrhyn Ychen **[3]**. Continue through the park and on the Coast Path. On leaving the park views open up of the cliffs ahead; the spectacular Needle Rock **[4]** is best viewed from here. Continue on past the stack to Fishguard fort **[5]** at Castle Point. From here continue to reach a parking bay (usually with ice cream van in summer).

8. From the car park follow the footpath adjacent to a wall, to shortly ascend stone steps leading up to the main road. Bear right and walk down to regain the start point.

FACILITIES
All available in the Fishguard area. Public toilets at the harbour (officially closed November to March, though I have seen them open during the winter season).

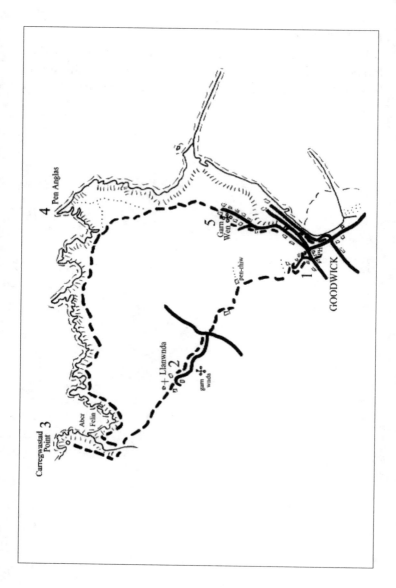

Pen Anglas 4

5 Garn Wen

GOODWICK

1

pen-rhiw

Llanwnda 2
garn wnda

Carregwastad Point 3
Aber Felin

13. Goodwick

6 miles/9.5 kilometres

OS Maps: 1:25 000 North Pembrokeshire Outdoor Leisure 35.
Start: Goodwick – car park adjacent to the Hope and Anchor.
Access: By Fishguard on the A40, and the A487 from St David's. Buses 404 the Strumble Shuttle between St David's and Newport, 410 Fishguard Town Service, 412 Haverfordwest to Cardigan, and 413 from St David's. Terminus for Irish ferry services and connecting rail link. Goodwick's railway station, closed in 1964, will re-open in 2012 with a brand new building and car park.
Parking: Car park adjacent to and in front of the Hope and Anchor Inn in the centre of Goodwick – signposted.
Grade: Moderate.

Hope and Anchor Inn (01348 872314)
www.hopeandanchorinn.co.uk
Opened in 1826 as the Sailors' Arms it became the Hope and Anchor with the arrival of a new landlord in the early 1860s. An attractive inn offering both food and accommodation. Bar and restaurants offer home cooking from local produce, with lots of nautical memorabilia to add to the atmosphere. Self catering and bed and breakfast available. Balcony overlooking the harbour.

HISTORY NOTES

1. Goodwick

Formerly a small fishing village Goodwick's development began with the creation of the harbour and the coming of the railway. Fishguard had been favoured by Brunel as the hub for rail and harbour services in the 1840s, Fishguard offering as it does the shortest crossing to Ireland from anywhere in England or Wales, however the Irish potato famine put a stop to plans. Neyland for a time was developed by Brunel as the terminal for Irish and transatlantic services, however by the end of the century Fishguard came back into favour with the Great Western Railway (GWR) management. Accordingly work began on building a suitable port here in 1899 – the rail track to Fishguard had finally been completed in this year. The cliffs above the prospective harbour were blasted not only to provide rock for the third of a mile long northern breakwater, but also to provide a platform for the new harbour and railway terminus, and necessary storage sheds. Houses were built on Goodwick's slopes for the new workforce at what is known as Harbour Village, and the mansion house overlooking the bay which had at one time been the home of an enterprising Minehead merchant and smuggler was rebuilt and extended to become in time the GWR's Fishguard Bay Hotel. The new harbour was operational by 1906, and with packet services to transfer from Neyland the steamer service to Rosslare was inaugurated, GWR steamers *St David*, *St Patrick* and *St George* sailing daily. As well as instigating services to Ireland Fishguard harbour had been built with the

Goodwick and Fishguard Harbour

expectation that it would develop as a rival to Liverpool, using Fishguard as the terminus for transatlantic sailings offered a saving of forty miles over New York to Liverpool. Accordingly Cunard, between 1910 and 1914, used Fishguard as the terminus for their New York sailings six to eight times monthly, with liners of the Booth and Blue Funnel lines also visiting. However with the outbreak of war, and silting of the harbour caused by the construction of a new breakwater in 1913, transatlantic sailings became fewer and fewer, and were not resumed after 1918. Stena Line continue to sail to Rosslare, whilst the B & I Line, who at one time operated from Fishguard, now run from Pembroke Dock to Rosslare. Goodwick played a role in aviation history when in April 1912 Denys Corbett Wilson made the first air flight to Ireland from Britain, flying his Bleriot from a field above Harbour Village. There are a series of floor mosaics along the Parrog (the flat section of the A40 between Fishguard and Goodwick town), illustrating aspects of Goodwick and Fishguard's history. Nowadays the village is popular as a holiday and boating centre. Goodwick Moor to the back of the Parrog, is fifteen acres of extensive reedbed, together with flood plain mire, scrub and a network of ditches. Plenty of bird life, with otters and water vole. There is a circular boardwalk through the reserve; access along the bridleway to the far side of the Seaview hotel, at the far end of the Parrog.

2. Llanwnda

The small hamlet of Llanwnda is the largest settlement on the Strumble/Pen Caer peninsula, dotted as it is with a typical pattern of small settlements and fields hedged by stone. The rocky outcrop of Garnwnda is boulder strewn, with on it's western side the Neolithic burial chamber of Garn Wnda. Dating from the 4th to early 3rd millennium BC it has a massive capstone resting partly on the ground, supported by a single upright. Excavations in the 19th century found a small urn containing bones. It's Celtic style church is dedicated to the 6th century St Gwyndaf. It has a double bellcote tower and leper's squint from the porch to the chancel. There are carved crosses cut into the outside wall of the chancel, and there is a carved face on one of the outer walls, which may be of the Virgin Mary, and

Llanwnda cross

may date from the 7th century. Inside there is a 15th century tonsured priest cut into one of the roof beams. The church was restored in 1870, partly rebuilt in 1881.

3. Carregwastad Point

Carregwastad is famous as the site of the last invasion of Britain in February 1797. The memorial stone was erected in 1897, in commemoration of the event. There is a 100 foot / 30.4 metres long tapestry depicting the events, and created as a community project for the second anniversary in 1997, on display in Fishguard Town Hall. The sheltered shingle beaches of Aber Felin bay are ideal for the local grey seals. Pupping takes place from September to December, with each female dropping a single pup, and the inaccessibility of the bay provides a safe and protected site. Good views north of the sloping flat top of Dinas Head, and on to Cemaes Head and Cardigan island.

ALLEZ FRANCE!

Following the great Revolution in France in 1789, the consequent Reign of Terror and the fall of Robespierre in 1794, power in France was administered from 1795 to 1799 by the Directory. Continuing the war begun in April 1792 against Austria the Directory devised a plan to deal with her two main enemies of the time: England and Austria. An English backed landing of French emigrés at Brittany in 1795 had been easily defeated by the Army of the West under General Lazare Hoche, one result of the victory being the acquisition of thousands of British uniforms and rifles which were to be used against England. It was proposed to conduct a war of privateers against the English, with landings on Irish and British soil to ferment anarchy and provide support for rebels.

In December 1796 Hoche's army of 15,000 left Brest for Bantry Bay in Ireland, but was unable to land, like the Spanish Armada of two hundred years or so before, because of storms. On 16 February 1797 a further expedition of 1400 men, the Légion Noire under the command of an Irish-American with experience of fighting in the American War of Independence, a Colonel Tate, left Brittany, bound for either Bristol or South Wales. Unable to land at Bristol the expedition of four ships sailed on, rounding St David's Head on Wednesday 22nd Februay 1797. Recognised, and forced out of Fishguard Bay by a single shot from Fishguard fort, it was decided to take advantage of the calm weather and moonlit night, and accordingly the men (in the now dyed British uniforms) and stores were landed at the steep cliffs of Carregwastad Point.

As planned the ships returned to France, while Colonel Tate set up his headquarters at Tre Howel farm. Transport and food now being the requirement the men – mainly grenadiers and ex-convicts – set out to scour Pencaer peninsula. January 1797 had seen a Portuguese coaster wrecked off the coast, and the majority of farms in the area had fine Portuguese wine in addition to cattle, pigs, poultry and sheep. Here the invasion started to go wrong, and the motley assortment of troops, making no attempt at concealment, decided to liberate the wine instead of the local populace. As a result several hundred of the invasion force deserted camp en masse.

By this time panic was spreading throughout the area, with both locals and French killed and injured. Fortunately the heroes of the hour were close at hand in the shape of Lord Cawdor of Stackpole and his Castlemartin Yeomanry, who, on hearing of the invasion, had marched north, collecting all able bodied men en route. They arrived at Fishguard early in the evening of the 23rd, ready to face the French, who were now deployed on the cliffs overlooking Goodwick. The night being particularly dark, the drums were sounded for recall, and Lord Cawdor's men retreated. The French, thinking the drums sounded the advance, also retreated, firing as they went. Stalemate.

Lord Cawdor's men in their blue uniforms had already been sighted by the French before they reached Fishguard, yet it is said the French also saw, silhouetted against the gun dark sky, another force dressed in red. These are believed to have been the local women who had gathered on the hills in their red cloaks, to act as spectators or soldiers as necessary. Cometh the hour, cometh the woman, and one Jemima Nicholas of Fishguard, not content to be a spectator, marched into battle with a pitchfork, rounded up twelve Frenchmen, and marched them off to Fishguard guardhouse.

The combination of events, desertions and dissatisfied officers had led Tate, by late on the Thursday evening, to sue for peace. Terms were agreed and the surrender signed on the morning of Friday 24th February 1797 at the Royal Oak in Fishguard – the table on which they signed is still there, with other memorabilia of events. The force accordingly marched down to Goodwick sands in the afternoon, and were escorted south to imprisonment in Haverfordwest's castle and churches. Among the French was James Bowen, formerly a servant at Tre Howel farm who had been transported for horse stealing, and who had joined the force at Brest. No doubt his presence had influenced the choice of Carregwastad Point, and the use of Tre Howel farm as the French headquarters.

All in all the Directory's campaign against England had proved to be a failure, as it had against Austria, that is with one notable exception. On the Italian Campaign General Napoleon Bonaparte swept all before him, a feat he was to repeat in 1799 when he swept the Directory away into European history, opening a new chapter in French – English relations.

4. Pen Anglas

The walk route runs inland across National Trust territory away from the headland of Pen Anglas, however the headland is famous and worth visiting for it's columnar jointing on it's north-eastern slope, just before the stone harbour marker. Similar, though not as spectacular as the Giant's Causeway or Fingal's Cave, it does show perhaps the finest cross section of jointing in dolerite on the British mainland. Much of the rock face has been divided into four, five or six sided columns, which while the overall surface is relatively smooth, their distinctiveness is easily discerned. Their appearance has given them their popular name of penny loaves. Formed during the cooling of molten rock contraction led to the production of the columns. The stone building with the blue doors once housed a Diaphone fog signal, the concrete pediments viewed along the route to Harbour Village carried poles for the power supply.

5. Garn Wen Neolithic burial chambers

Dating from the 4th to early 3rd millennium BC three burial chambers are set in a line running north to south behind the houses of Harbour Village. The southern-most is the best preserved, it's capstone resting partly on the ground and partly on three low stone uprights. The chambers are typical of a number of similar such chambers on the Strumble Head peninsula which use large flat slabs for construction, and which are sited below prominent rock outcrops. Garn Wen's chambers would have had fine views over Fishguard Bay.

WALK DIRECTIONS [-] indicates history note

1. Starting from the car park walk up the steps to the north of the car park, between the surgery and the inn, to gain the main routes through Goodwick town [1]. Cross and take the steps and path leading up to the right of the Glendower hotel. Route signposted.

2. Once at a minor road bear left and almost

immediately right uphill. Ignore a path leading off to the left over a footbridge and continue to the top of the road. Go past Pen Cwm cottage, and before the next house bear left onto a signposted bridleway.

3. Ignore paths leading off right and left and go ahead until the path becomes a farm track leading to Pen-rhiw. Once at Pen-rhiw bear left and continue on a farm track, passing Llanwnda Stables, to reach a minor road.

4. Cross the road and continue ahead on the road down to Llanwnda [2]. There are two signposted public footpaths on the left en route, initially along tarmac and leading to houses – these will make for a circular walk around Garnwnda, or using link paths over the top of it for some great views; the burial chamber is on it's western flank, the second footpath will take you quickly there and back before continuing on down to Llanwnda; just past two houses there is a clear path leading off left, the chamber visible above just below the summit.

5. At the cross roads in Llanwnda continue ahead, the church is immediately on your right. Continue ahead past church and houses to join access paths leading by lane and field to the Coast Path; well waymarked. Once at the Coast Path bear left and cross Cwm Felin to reach the memorial marker to the last invasion of Britain at Carregwastad Point [3].

6. Retrace your steps to Cwm Felin and continue on the Coast Path to reach the access gate to the National Trust owned Pen Anglas [4]. Choice here to continue ahead on the Coast Path, or to cut across to the headland of Pen Anglas. From Pen Anglas it is possible to cut back to rejoin the Coast Path, or to follow a coastal path until it

rejoins the Coast Path further along.

7. Continue to reach Harbour Village. After the first house on the right immediately bear right onto a public footpath, initially tarmac, and pass to the right of the garages and almost immediately, just past a hedge, bear left onto a path. Continue on this path, ignoring higher paths, to walk past the burial chambers of Garn Wen [5].

8. Emerging at a car park continue to the road, bear left and then right, and continue downhill on the road. Keep a lookout for a gap in the wall on the left, where the Coast Path, waymarked, will carry you by a zig zag path down to the access road to the Fishguard Bay hotel.

9. Bear right and continue, keeping a look out for the Coast Path route, which waymarked, leads down steps on the left, onto a path leading you across a metal footbridge over the main access road to the ferry. Once across bear right and continue to the main road leading you back right to Goodwick and the starting point.

FACILITIES

All available in Goodwick and Fishguard. Dating from 1827 the Rose and Crown adjacent to the Hope and Anchor is currently closed; plans are in place for it to re-open in 2012. Goodwick's Parrog has the Celtic Diving Base and the Tourist Information Centre, with it's own café and the Ocean Lab. Public toilets on the Parrog. There is a marine walk linking Goodwick with Fishguard; terrain easy, with lots of benches, ascend the hill at the end of the Parrog and follow the cliff top lane on the left. There are currently plans in consideration to develop Fishguard Harbour as a mixed use marina with new residential apartments which will considerably alter the appearance and facilities of the waterfront.

14. mathry and aber mawr

5.75 miles/9.25 kilometres

OS Maps: 1:25 000 North Pembrokeshire Outdoor Leisure 35.
Start: Farmers Arms in Mathry.
Access: Mathry is located on a hill just off the A487 Fishguard to St David's road. Buses 413 Fishguard to St David's Monday to Saturday, and 404 The Strumble Shuttle daily May to September, less frequently in winter.
Parking: Small car park for patrons by the Farmers Arms, with plenty of other parking possible in the village. Small parking bay near to the church.
Grade: Moderate.

The Farmers Arms, Mathry (01348 831284)
www.farmersarmsmathry.co.uk

An old traditional pub dating from at least the 1860s the Farmers is set in the middle of the village. It's cosy interior is complemented by, outback, a covered garden area. Bougainvillea, passion flowers

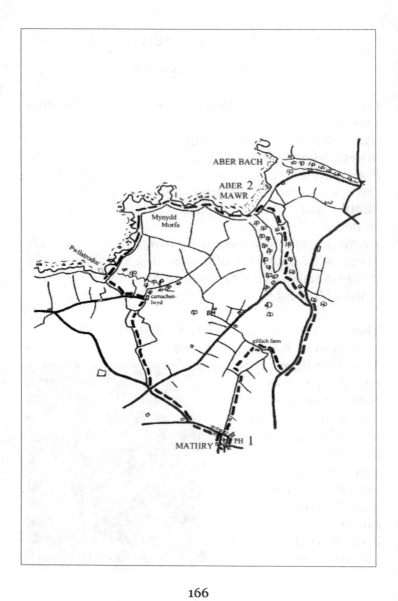

ABER BACH

ABER 2
MAWR

Mynydd
Morfa

Pwllstrodur

carnachenlwyd

gilfach farm

MATHRY PH 1

and honeysuckle vie for space with home grown grapes, which when red and ripe taste sweet and could make for a sweet dessert! Wine has been made with them, but a slightly different atmosphere would be needed to make this an ongoing concern. Open all day in the summer season. Food available, locally sourced where possible.

HISTORY NOTES
1. Mathry
Mathry is a fine example of a medieval hilltop village, though there would certainly have been earlier settlements. It's dominant position in the area made it an ideal choice for trade and commerce, and markets and fairs were held here for centuries; the right to hold them nationally regularised by charter under Edward III in the 14th century. The closeness of the name Mathry to the word martyr – in Welsh *merthyr*, in Latin *martyrium* – led to a fanciful tale as told in the 12th century Welsh *Book of Llandaff*. On one day a Pembrokeshire woman gave birth to seven sons; a source of joy and wonder to the mother perhaps, but one of sorrow to the father, who, unable to support them, vowed to drown them in the river Taf. However they were saved in the nick of time by St Teilo, who baptised them and took them away with him, each of them being henceforth provided for by the daily appearance of a large fish by the water's edge. After tutelage by Saints Teilo and Dyfrig the seven were sent by St Teilo to Mathry where they lived until their deaths, becoming known in the meantime as the seven saints of Mathry. The church is accordingly dedicated to the seven saints.

The present church dates from 1869, though there would have been earlier buildings on site. The churchyard is roughly circular, and many very early Celtic churches were set in circular churchyards, however in this case it may indicate an even earlier Iron Age settlement. At one time the belfry was topped by a steeple, a handy inland navigation marker for passing ships out at sea. In the church porch is a 5th or 6th century stone pillar with a dedication to *Maccuoicci filius* (son) *of Caticuus* in Latin. It's ogham inscription, an Irish script developed by the 5th century, is indecipherable. Two stones set in the outer churchyard wall to the right of the gate are incised with crosses. One was formally serving as a gatepost, the other part of a farmhouse wall.

2. Aber Mawr

The approach to Aber Mawr is through Pen yr Allt and Broom woods, pleasant woods of oak, ash, and hazel, carpeted during spring with bluebells and wild garlic. During the Mesolithic period this wooded landscape would have stretched far out to sea, but as sea levels rose the land disappeared beneath the waters. The fossilised remnants of this forest can be seen at low tides. The storm beach of shingle and stone is more recent, having been thrown up during a ferocious storm in 1859 which destroyed well over a hundred ships in it's wild passage across land and sea. That well known Victorian in his stove pipe hat was here in the 1840s, Isambard Kingdom Brunel was hatching another engineering feat on behalf of the Great Western Railway (GWR). It was planned to run the South Wales Railway, formed in 1844 as small brother and project of the GWR, from Cardiff to

Aber Mawr

Swansea, Carmarthen and Fishguard, to connect with steamboats for Ireland. Then, in 1846, came the terrible Irish potato famine and the proposed route to Fishguard was scrapped.

Then, for some reason, whether it was Aber Mawr's softer rock, or the fact that payment from the GWR was to be paid only on completion of the railway, Brunel shifted his proposed terminus to Aber Mawr. Abutments for piers were built at Penmorfa and Carreg Golchfa, the two headlands that enclose Aber Mawr and Aber Bach, and an incline for rail track laid down; the traces are still there for the keen-eyed. However, in 1851, as soon as he had arrived, Brunel was gone, work abandoned, and Neyland chosen as the new terminal. Connection was made with Ireland eventually – a submarine telegraph cable was laid across the Irish Sea in 1883 from what is now a private dwelling by Aber Bach's parking bay. Fishguard had to wait until 1906 before she got her Irish ferry connection. Aber Mawr and Aber Bach are now popular and uncrowded beaches, both good for swimming and exploration.

WALK DIRECTIONS [-] indicates history note

1. Starting from the Farmers Arms in Mathry [1] pass in front of the pub entrance and keeping pub and church on your left follow the road as it heads up left to meet the road through Mathry to Abercastle – the church entrance is to your left. Bear right onto the road leading out of Mathry, but almost immediately bear right again and go between houses – the two by the road marked *Pen yr Idlan* and *Hen Bwthyn* – and continue to gain a track.

2. Follow the track, until just by a house the route enters a field. Continue across two fields, keeping hedge to your left, to enter a third. Bear left. In the middle of the field, away from the hedge, is a fenced off lane heading downhill. Follow this down and go between barns to meet a T junction. Ignore the green lane leading off left, but bear right to enter the yard of Gilfach farm through a farm gate, and keeping the house on your left continue on a concrete trackway to meet the B road leading down to Aber Mawr.

3. Bear left. Ignore a road bearing off left but continue ahead to shortly meet a path bearing off left through woodland. National Trust sign here for Broom Wood, together with signpost of walking man, and a small holly tree.

4. Stay ahead on this path, ignoring a stile leading off left some way along the route, and another path further along bearing right uphill. Finally meet a level path and bear right. Continue to reach a kissing gate and enter an

open field. Continue ahead to reach another kissing gate giving access to Aber Mawr [2].

5. Bear left and continue on the Coast Path across the head of the beach, heading up steps, and following the Path as it bears initially right and then left around Mynydd Morfa to reach the sheltered and pretty cove of Pwllstrodur.

6. Cross the footbridge here and follow the Coast Path as it bears up and right to reach a stile and signpost indicating Public Footpath to the left. Do not cross the stile but bear left uphill and keep fence, hedge and small stream on your right to reach a metal gate at the top right of the field giving access to a tarmac road.

7. Bear left and continue to Carnachen-lwyd. Go ahead keeping the house on your left and almost immediately bear right to gain a bridleway heading out across a field. Cross this field keeping to the left edge, to reach another gate giving access to another field. Enter this field and head out across the middle of the field aiming for the right angled field corner opposite. Once here bear uphill, keeping hedge on your immediate right.

8. At the top right hand corner meet a green lane and follow this to meet a tarmac road. Bear left and continue directly uphill and ahead to reach Mathry. Once back in Mathry either bear left just before the church, or continue past the church to bear left and continue back to the starting point.

FACILITIES
Most available in Mathry. Public toilets closed November to March.

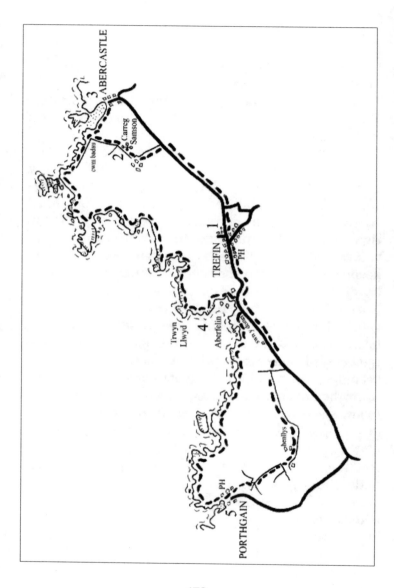

15. trefin and abercastle

7.75 miles/12.5 kilometres

Note: Can be broken down into two shorter walks, the Trefin Abercastle section and the Aberfelin Porthgain section. Alternatively combine with walk 16 to make a longer walk.

OS Maps: 1:25 000 North Pembrokeshire Outdoor Leisure 35.
Start: The Ship Inn in Trefin.
Access: Trefin is on the minor road between St David's and Abercastle, easily accessible from the A487 St David's to Goodwick road. Bus 404 The Strumble Shuttle, St David's to Fishguard and vice versa, daily May to September, Mondays, Thursdays and Saturdays only during winter. 413 St David's to Fishguard Mondays to Saturdays.
Parking: Large car park at the Ship for patrons. Plenty of parking space in the village. Parking also possible at Abercastle and Porthgain.
Grade: Moderate.

The Ship Inn, 35 Ffordd y Felin, Trefin (01348 831445)

Family friendly and family owned pub, which has for much of it's history been associated with the Maddocks family. Dating back to at least 1805 it's first landlady was unfortunate in losing three of her family to the sea. The Ship is children and dog friendly, offering four rooms to choose from – open fires for colder days. Attractive lawned beer garden to the rear, with good views over open country. Homemade food and real ales. The anchor outside the front entrance is reputedly from the Ragna, a three masted sailing ship wrecked off Aberfelin in 1900 with the loss of eight lives, though many of the crew were pulled to safety by villagers.

HISTORY NOTES
1. Trefin
Trefin is the largest village between Fishguard and St David's. It is a medieval settlement, probably dating from the late 12th or early 13th century, and founded by one of the Norman bishops. There was a Bishop's Palace here, though where it was sited is uncertain. The houses along it's linear pattern of settlement are mostly late 19th century, many built directly onto rock, this rock protruding at it's village 'green' on it's eastern side. Part of it resembles a seat, and on here at one time Trefin's mock mayor was installed every November. The village pump survives.

2. Carreg Samson
Dated to the 4th to early 3rd millennium BC this superb Neolithic burial chamber is one of the finest in the county. Only three of it's remaining six pillars now support the capstone of over 16ft/5m by 9ft/3m. Originally the whole structure would have been covered; it is not certain by what but it may have been clay subsoil. Excavation in 1968 suggested that uprights and capstone were constructed over a pit, and that there had been a passage leading into the chamber, making this

one of many passage graves found in the west of the UK. Burial here was by cremation. Local tradition has it that the capstone was lifted into place by Samson using his little finger – the Samson in question may have been St Samson, the 6th century Abbot of Caldey island, rather than the strongman of the Bible. This extravagant action did him no good for in the process he lost his finger. In memoriam the finger was buried on Ynys Castell

Carreg Samson

(*Castle island*), the island guarding Abercastle's right flank, in what is known as the grave of Samson's finger. Longhouse farm, on which the burial chamber is sited, was once a grange of the Bishop of St David's, whose Palace, as noted under Trefin, is now untraceable.

3. Abercastle

The small valley leading down from Carreg Samson to Abercastle is named Cwm Badau (*valley of the boats*), but at one time it was also used to describe the cove of Abercastle with it's pretty colour washed cottages. Hard to believe now, but this was once a bustling little sea port, known as a safe harbour as far back as 1566. In the early 19th century out by local sloop went exports of corn

Abercastle

and butter to Bristol, returning from there with general merchandise. Coal and limestone were landed for the harbour's limekiln. Perhaps also the occasional ship called in from Liverpool. There were three vessels ranging from 25 to 34 tons built here between 1790 and 1820; perhaps they added a little smuggling to supplement their legitimate cargoes. The farmlands around Mathry are noted as some of the richest in the county, and coal and culm, and perhaps imported anthracite, were used to fire the limekiln at the head of the beach to provide the lime needed to sweeten the soil. There are two mooring bollards on the Coast Path leading away from Abercastle which once saw service as canons and which were taken from a French frigate that foundered nearby, one by the limekiln, the other at Cwm Badau. The ruined building on the headland to the right is the old granary. Coastal trade continued until the 1920s, when road transport came into the ascendancy.

Abercastle is nowadays a sailing and shell fishing harbour, popular with divers, many of it's homes holiday cottages. Sadly of it's three former pubs none remain. Ynys Castell, sheltering the cove, may have been an early Christian site, and is accessible at low tides.

FIRST SAILING ACROSS THE ATLANTIC

On 10th August 1876 a young man sailed into Abercastle so weak that he had to be carried from his fishing dory. He was Alfred Johnson. Originally from Denmark he had run away to sea as a teenager, and after working on square riggers had ended up as a fisherman in Gloucester, Massachusetts, USA. Sometime in 1874 he had been discussing with friends whether a single handed crossing of the Atlantic was possible, and he had asserted that it was and that it could be done in a dory, a small shallow draft boat used for fishing. He also said that he could do it, and keeping to his word spent $200 on a specially designed dory he named *Centennial* in honour of the United States' first centennial. His voyage would be a celebration of it. Accordingly he set sail on 15th June in his 20 foot/6.1 metre dory, painted red, white and blue, and with the Stars and Stripes flying from the masthead was seen off from Gloucester by a large crowd. After a brief stop in Nova Scotia, and a capsizing in August, he duly arrived, by chance, in Abercastle to restock his provisions. After two days rest he continued on to his final destination at

Liverpool, where he arrived to an enthusiastic welcome. Johnson stayed in Liverpool for several months, where he exhibited his boat, returning home with his dory aboard the passenger steamer *Greece*, arriving in New York in February 1877. His feat earned him the nickname *Centennial*, and with his dory he toured several cities to tell his story, however the tour did not generate as much interest as he had hoped. He returned to fishing, and to the captaincy of a vessel. In 2003 a slate plaque in honour of Johnson's feat was unveiled by his grandson Charles Dickman, it is housed in the slipway wall. *Centennial* is now housed at the Cape Ann Historical Museum in Gloucester, Massachusetts.

4. Aberfelin and Trefin mill

Aberfelin is Trefin's beach, attractive, though rocky and with shingle. It was a busy place when the mill was running, and when the cove was used by both quarrymen and fishermen. A quarry was started on the headland at Trwyn Llwyd in the late 1860s, remaining in operation until closure in 1887. Many of the quarrymen and local fishermen lived in the row of 19th century cottages nearby, now listed as *Y Cwm* (the valley). The mill was in use for at least some five hundred years, Trefin's villagers bringing sacks of wheat for milling into flour for bread, with barley for grinding into animal feed. By the beginning of the 20th century, with improvements in land transport, cheap grain began to be imported and milled in the larger town mills. This competition spelt the end for Trefin mill, and like many similar mills throughout the land, closure was inevitable, and came in 1918. The mill became the focus for one of the Welsh language's finest lyrics when, in 1918 just after closure, poet and Archdruid Crwys wrote, in rough translation, *the mill does not grind tonight, at Trefin beside the sea, but no one grinds here any more, save sullen time* ... The leat which supplied the mill with it's water still runs.

5. Porthgain

A fascinating place to while away a few hours Porthgain is unique in the history of Pembrokeshire's coastal settlements. It's industrial buildings and harbour gives it it's flavour, and it is still a working fishing port. Full history under the Porthgain and Abereiddi walk – walk 16.

WALK DIRECTIONS [-] indicates history note

1. Starting from the Ship in Trefin [1] walk up through the village and continue ahead on the Abercastle road. At the walled entrance to Longhouse farm bear left to bear right by the farmhouse, and passing Carreg Samson [2] on your right, continue to reach the Coast Path.

2. Bear right and continue on the path to Abercastle [3]. From Abercastle retrace your steps, but remain on the Coast Path and follow it, ignoring any footpaths leading off it, to reach the ruins of Trefin mill at Aberfelin [4]. Just before turning towards Aberfelin, on the headland of Trwyn Llwyd, are the ruins of the old quarry.

3. Bear right at the road, and crossing the bridge continue uphill on the minor road. Ignore the first

indicated footpath turning onto the Coast Path at Swn y Don, and continue on the road, passing Awel-For on the right, and just past here bear right through a kissing gate, and bearing diagonally left cross a field reach another kissing gate.

4. Continue across the field keeping the hedge to your left to meet a green lane. Continue, passing Henllys on your right, and follow the track around left and right until just before a large house above left bear right onto the first signposted route at a gate. Continue the short distance ahead right to a metal kissing gate.

5. Go ahead across the field and continue through kissing gates to cross right a stream by a wooden footbridge. Bear left once across and continue ahead into Porthgain [5]. Continue down to the harbour to bear right onto the Coast Path by a limekiln. Continue until the path joins the minor road to Trefin at Swn y Don. Bear left to return to Trefin.

FACILITIES

Hand weaving centre, craft shop and tea room next to the pub in Trefin. Youth hostel in the village. Public toilets at Abercastle (closed November to mid February) – situated behind the building on the left, just before the slipway. Toilets and BT phone at Porthgain, as well as Bistro, the Sloop Inn and art galleries.

16. porthgain and abereiddi

3.5 miles/5 kilometres

Note: Can be combined with the Trefin and Abercastle walk to make for a longer outing.

OS Maps: 1:25 000 North Pembrokeshire Outdoor Leisure 35.
Start: Porthgain's car park, in front of the Sloop Inn.
Access: Porthgain is situated on the coast roughly halfway between Fishguard and St David's. From the A487 at Croesgoch follow the minor road through Llanrhian. Bus 404 the Strumble Shuttle Fishguard to St David's calls at Porthgain, as does the 413 on schooldays.
Parking: Spacious car park in Porthgain.
Grade: Easy.

The Sloop Inn, Porthgain (01348 831449)
www.sloop.co.uk
Bigger on the inside than it looks the Sloop Inn has long been a Pembrokeshire favourite. Lots of outside seating in what can be a suntrap in summer. A pub and restaurant the Sloop is open all day from 09.30 serving breakfast, lunch and dinner. Often fresh fish and local lobster in season. Inside the interior is brick, slate and quarry tile, with lots of local memorabilia around the walls, including a striking portrait of Porthgain's first engine, the *Porthgain*, which worked the quarries above the village. The inn probably dates from 1851 when a

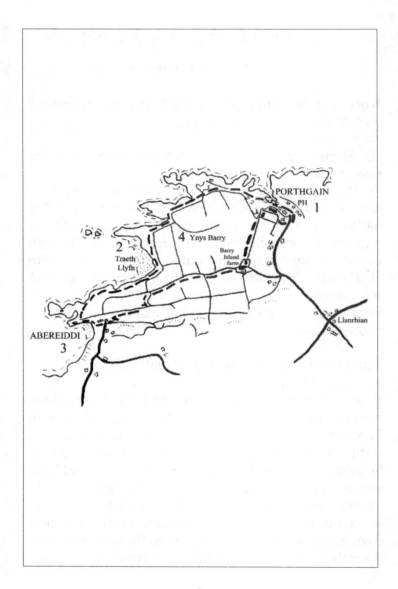

local agricultural labourer, Benjamin George, turned his cottage into an ale house to serve the quarry workers and help finance his family of seven children (though there is a sign inside the pub stating 1743). Children and dogs welcome.

HISTORY NOTES
1. Porthgain
Anyone visiting Porthgain for the first time will immediately be aware of the imposing ruins marching up the cliff face from the harbour. A visitor 160 years or so ago would have seen none of this, perhaps only a huddle of fishing boats drawn up on a different shoreline, for Porthgain's harbour owes it's present shape to man-made construction. Porthgain's geology has given the area an identity and industrial history unique in Pembrokeshire. The metamorphosed shale here gave slate for flooring and roofing, the clay was used for brick making, and the volcanic dolerite rock provided roadstone for Britain's developing roads. Porthgain's industrial revolution started in 1837 when George Le Hunte, the local landowner, granted a lease to a local company to extract flags, slates and stones. However it was a London consortium, Barclay & Company, who were granted other leases in 1840, who started the transformation. The first harbour was built, the first quarries were developed, and the first tramway joining nearby Abereiddi and it's slate quarry to Porthgain harbour was laid. Brick making had to wait until 1878, when, under the St Brides Slate & Slab Co., Porthgain's heavier than normal bricks began to find

their way to places as far afield as Dublin and Bridgwater. By 1912, after several changes of ownership, there were three steam locomotives, plus traction engines and motor lorry, on site. One loco, the *Charger*, had seen service in the Jarrow shipyards, the others were the *Singapore*, and appropriately, as first engine, the *Porthgain*.

Porthgain

The slate and brick industries here fell into decline by the early 1900s, and crushed stone took on greater importance. Small pieces of blasted stone were hauled up the *Jerusalem Road* from Porthgain's quarry and crushed into sizes from 0.25 to 2.5 inches and stored in the hoppers. They were then exported by company ship or road. By 1931 fortunes declined, and in August of that year business closed. There are still extensive ruins worth exploration. The present restaurant was the former company offices, and Ty Mawr, the recently restored building adjacent to the green, was connected with brick making. The stone chutes and hoppers dominate the harbour, and the old tunnel cut through to Porthgain's slate quarry can be easily picked out. On the cliffs above are the ruins of the former quarrymen's cottages, and the loco shed, weighbridge and water tower still partially stand. The extensive quarry and ruined smithy can be explored from the *Jerusalem Road*. The village is now in local ownership, with the harbour, quarries and cliff land the responsibility of the National Park.

2. Traeth Llyfn

Traeth Llyfn, translated as the smooth, or sleek beach, does have a fine sandy beach. Good for swimming, though there is a strong outgoing current, noticeably to the left. From the headlands around Traeth Llyfn the rock outcrops of Carn Llidi and Pen Beri appear as truly imposing mountains dominating St David's Head. St Finbar is said to have sailed from here to found the city of Cork, while Columba sailed en route to Iona.

3. Abereiddi

The slate quarry here at Abereiddi was part and parcel of Porthgain's industrial enterprise. The poor harbour, vessels of only twenty to thirty tons could load from the quarry slip, meant that the construction of a tramway to Porthgain harbour was essential. In length just under two miles, trains, consisting of usually two or three wagons, were hauled by two horses to the Slate Yard near Barry Island farm for storage, before being shipped out. The quarry was at it's busiest from circa 1850 to

1904, with exports of Abereiddi and Porthgain slate to Bristol Channel and English Channel ports. The ruins of the engine house, the dressing sheds, and the quarrymen's cottages known as The Row, are still evident. Sometime after quarrying had ceased the connecting walls leading from the old engine house around to the dressing sheds were blasted away, resulting in a small harbour, well known locally as *The Blue Lagoon* – the water truly is blue! The bay is famous in geological circles for the fossil graptolites found in it's Ordovician slates when split. A first was recorded here with the discovery of a previously unknown example of these plant-like animals. There is a possibly 18th century observation tower on Trwyn Castell head overlooking Abereiddi bay. A curious building, there is even a fireplace inside should you need to warm up. Like many remote headlands on the Pembrokeshire coast Trwyn Castell would have been home to Iron Age settlers.

4. Ynys Barry (*Barry island*)

Barry island takes it's name from a geological feature of the landscape, hinted at by the narrow valley along which the tramway from Abereiddi ran. As the Ice Age came to an end the Irish Sea ice melted, and a sub glacial meltwater channel was formed which ran down to Abereiddi bay and provided temporary island status. Dinas island (more properly Dinas Head), near Newport, owes it's landscape charter to similar action.

WALK DIRECTIONS [-] indicates history note

1. From the car park in Porthgain [1] walk down to the harbour to pass the old stone chutes. By the stone

building (the former Pilot House) climb the steps to reach the headland. To the right, on the headland, there is a stone pillar, matched by another on the opposite side of the harbour. These mark the harbour entrance.

2. Continue ahead. After a short distance the path breaks in two. Keep to the left hand path – the right, known as the *Jerusalem Road*, leads downhill to the old quarry and the ruins of the smithy. Keep to the level path, passing to the left above the quarry, and follow the Coast Path to Traeth Llyfn [2]. Metal steps lead down to this popular beach.

3. Continue on the Coast Path as it bears right around the beach headland, and follow it on to Abereiddi [3] – bear right on a level path before heading down to the beach to reach the Blue Lagoon. Once at Abereiddi proper head inland from the beach, keeping the ruined quarrymen's cottages on your immediate left, to reach a path by the public toilets.

4. Cross into the field ahead. Keep to the top of the slope and continue ahead to reach a wooden stile. Cross and keeping to the right field edge continue to a field gate. Ignore the stile in front of you – this leads back to the coast – and instead continue right on a farm track.

5. Follow the farm track across Ynys Barry [4] to Barry Island farm and bear left just after the farm buildings on a signposted track. Keeping to the right and then left of fields reach a path bearing right back to Porthgain and the starting point – left would take you back to the headland above the harbour.

FACILITIES

Parking is also possible at Abereiddi, where there are public toilets, emergency telephone, and seasonal ice cream van. Bistro in Porthgain, as well as two art galleries, public telephone and toilets.

17. St David's and Porth Clais

6 miles/9.5 kilometres

OS Maps: 1:25 000 North Pembrokeshire Outdoor Leisure 35.

Start: Farmers' Arms in Goat Street St David's.

Access: St David's is at the end of the A487 Haverfordwest and Fishguard roads. Buses 342, 400 (the Puffin Shuttle), 404 (the Strumble Shuttle), 411 and 413 all stop at St David's. Local city bus 403 the Celtic Coaster calls at Porth Clais in season.

Parking: There is free parking in the Pebbles (the road leading down to the cathedral from Cross Square). Other signposted car parks in and around St David's. Parking also possible at Caerfai Bay and Porth Clais.

Grade: Moderate.

The Bishops, Cross Square, St David's (01437 720422)

A new comer to St David's this former hotel offers plenty of menu choice, both inside and in the tiered garden area to the rear. Two buildings joined together with the addition of an extension at the back gives the Bishops lots of space. Closed during the winter season.

The Farmers' Arms, Goat St, St David's (01437 720328) www.farmersstdavids.co.uk

Possibly created out of two former cottages, one a confectionery shop, the Farmers' now comprises three rooms, one a dining area. There is a roomy patio

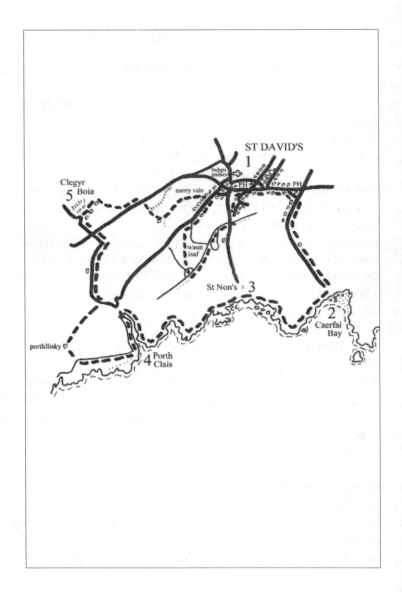

outback, a regular suntrap in summer. The pub has been dated back to at least 1835, and until recently was the only surviving pub in the city. The present structure of the pub, with it's exposed stonework, more open area and patio date back to changes instigated by new landlords from 1986. As much a locals as visitors pub the Farmers' stays open all day with a varied lunchtime and evening menu.

The Grove Hotel, High St, St David's (01437 720341) www.grovestdavids.co.uk
At one time a town house and then a private school the Grove began life as a pub hotel in about 1870 when a local entrepreneur took over and developed the business. Part of the business included a horse drawn omnibus known as *The Duke*, and which collected visitors from Haverfordwest. Now more a hotel than a pub the Grove has been refurbished and extended, with conservatories added. There is a fine walled garden. Open all day. Locally sourced food from their own vegetable and herb garden. Winner of the Welsh Assembly's Climate Pub Challenge in 2009 energy saving is part of it's ethos.

HISTORY NOTES
1. St David's

St David founded his church and monastery in the mid 6th century, though nothing remains of the foundations. Property was held in common, with emphasis on prayer and simple sustenance through water and a primarily vegetarian diet. David himself is believed to have travelled widely before establishing his community, helping to establish centres at Glastonbury, Bath and Gloucester, and, according to legend, travelling to Jerusalem in the company of other local saints where he was given an altar stone by the Patriarch. He died March 1st possibly in 589 or 601. The settlement survived the frequent Viking raids, but it's importance was seen as a threat by the incoming Normans, who imposed their own pattern of cathedral and diocese. William the Conqueror paid homage here in 1081. According to tradition David himself was canonized by Pope Calixtus II in 1123. The present cathedral, Wales' finest church, was begun in 1181, reaching it's final building phase by the early 16th century when the tower was raised to it's present height by Bishop Vaughan. There is a fine and unique oak ceiling in the nave, it's initial phase of construction dating from the 1530s. It is of Renaissance styling, and has been attributed to Flemish craftsmen. Recent examination of the roof has suggested that it is of Welsh oak. Poor foundations and a 13th century earthquake has caused the west wall of the nave and it's arcade pillars to lean outwards; thus a wooden ceiling rather than a stone vault. Of the delightful carvings under the Choir misericords (ledged seats allowing

St David's Cathedral

infirm priests support during offices which required them to stand) twenty-one can be dated to approximately the late 15th century; the seven others are Victorian replacements. They offer a fine commentary on medieval life, humour and imagination. The original cathedral city would have been surrounded by a 14th century wall interspersed with four gatehouses; the Tower Gatehouse is the only one to survive. Pilgrims, arriving by road and sea, flocked to St David's throughout the Middle Ages. On the pilgrimage route from Ireland to Santiago de Compostela in Spain via Wales, Cornwall and Brittany, it was said that two pilgrimages to St David's was equal to one to Rome, three the equal of one to Jerusalem. Following the Reformation the cathedral nearly fell into ruin, requiring

Cathedral misericord

restoration in 1763, and again between 1862 and 1877 when Gilbert Scott redesigned the west front more in accord with it's medieval appearance. New cloisters were built between 2004 and 2007. St David's is unique in that the reigning sovereign is a canon of the cathedral and chapter. The ruined Bishop's Palace nearby was largely built between 1280 and 1350 by Bishop Gower. Abetted by the Reformation the Palace was derelict by the 18th century. Recognising St David's continuing importance it was awarded city status in 1995; it is the United Kingdom's smallest city.

2. Caerfai Bay

Caerfai has a fine stretch of sand at low tides, making it St David's local beach. Popular with locals and visitors it's cliffs also afford space for coasteers, the sport that combines swimming with cliff exploration – jumping off the rocks into the sea is part of the fun. Along with neighbouring Caer Bwdy it's quarries provided it's distinctive purplish stone for the cathedral; nearby Caer

Bwdy's quarry was re-opened as recently as 1996 when sufficient stone was quarried for repair work for the cathedral's west front and any future building work.

3. St Non's

St David was born here, reputedly in a thunderstorm, on the site now occupied by St Non's chapel, in around 520. It is said that Non's Well sprang forth at his birth. St Non, the saint's mother, went to Brittany shortly after the birth. Her tomb is in the chapel of Dirinon in Finistère. His father was reputed to be Sant, a Ceredigion chief. St Non's Retreat was built in 1929, the Chapel of Our Lady and St Non in 1934.

4. Porth Clais

Porth Clais has always been the harbour for St David's, and was at one time under the ownership of the church – *porth* is the Welsh word for port, *clais*, it has been argued, stands for a monastic community. St David was baptized here at the head of the creek by Elvis, Bishop of Munster; there is a well on the site, where at one time it is believed a chapel also stood. Cathedral records show coal and limestone being landed here as early as 1384. Caerfai and Caer Bwdi's purple stone was landed here for the cathedral, as was the oak for the roof of the nave. Later imports included general merchandise and timber from Ireland, with exports of corn, malt and wool. Bristol became a much favoured port of call with local corn going to help feed the city's growing population. Ships, most with purpose built flat bottoms, would have been beached here and their cargoes unloaded onto waiting carts. There is in the cathedral a misericord carving of a typical 14th and 15th century cargo ship of the type that would have visited Porth Clais being repaired by shipwrights. The breakwater, possibly Norman in origin, was extensively repaired in the 18th century. The lime kilns on the old trading quays would have been in constant use. The limestone burnt in the kilns was taken by horse and cart for spreading on the fields, and for use as mortar. Lime as mortar was used in the construction of the cathedral, though the lime for this would probably have been burnt in kilns at the cathedral site. The restored kilns here were in constant use from 1650 to 1900. As well as providing a safe haven for trade and shelter Porth Clais' natural harbour was favoured by the occasional marauding Norseman, intent on sacking St David's semi-monastic settlement. The Mabinogion, that gem of medieval Welsh tales, notes Porth Clais as the landing place of the mythical boar, Twrch Trwyth, hotly pursued by Arthur. Later more materialistic ages would have seen the odd smuggler or two, often combining his activities with legitimate trade. The last imports to the harbour were of coal, required up to the 1950s to supply the city's gasworks, now demolished, and which stood on the site of the present car park. The inlet is still a busy place, popular now with the outdoor enthusiast, whether water borne or rock climber.

5. Clegyr Boia (*Boia's Rock*)

Boia was an Irish chieftain and contemporary of St David who built his stronghold on the rock outcrop overlooking the peninsula. He came into conflict with St David when David decided to move his religious house from the shadow of Carn Llidi, the rock outcrop at St

David's Head, to the banks of the river Alun. Legend has it that Boia's wife taunted St David and the local monks by having her maids disport themselves in the river *with bodies bare*. Undeterred St David finally persuaded Boia to grant him the land on which the cathedral now stands. Boia himself was killed and his stronghold destroyed by a fellow Irish chieftain Lisci or Lysgi, who gives his name to Porthlysgi Bay around the coast from Porth Clais.

Excavations undertaken here in 1902 and 1942 showed that the site had been in occupation during the Neolithic period. Traces of timber huts, pottery, stone axes and flint scrapers were found – it is one of the very few Neolithic settlements to have been found in Wales. The settlers here may well have made use of the two burial chambers to be found at Carn Llidi and St David's Head. Archaeologists have determined how a Neolithic house built on the hill would have looked – set between two rock walls it's wooden roof would have been supported by eight timber posts. Excavation also showed that the site was in use at a later date, possibly Iron Age, or possibly it is Boia's settlement. Built in the early Iron Age tradition, stone faced ramparts would have enclosed the hill top. The gate, sited on the south-western slope, was found on excavation to have guard recesses on it's inner side. Well worth taking the short track to the summit for the superb views of the landscape, with the cathedral tucked away safely in the valley of Merry Vale.

WALK DIRECTIONS [-] indicates history note

1. Starting from the Farmers' Arms in Goat Street head into the centre of St David's [1], and passing the city's

14th century cross (restored in the 1870s) continue up High Street. Bear right into Feidr Pant-y-Bryn (*hollow of the hill lane*) – the Tourist Information Centre to your left is worth a visit, both for it's architectural design and it's art gallery, shop and café. The Grove is opposite the Centre.

2. At the end of the lane turn right into the Caerfai road and continue on to Caerfai Bay [2]. From the car park head down steps to join the Coast Path and continue right, via St Non's [3], to reach Porth Clais [4].

3. At Porth Clais continue on the Coast Path, past the restored lime kilns, to reach a kissing gate on the headland. Choice of two paths – take the right hand path and continue ahead with the fence to your immediate right. The Coast Path heads off to the left.

4. Where the path bears left turn right to reach a farm gate. Go ahead on a permissive path to reach Porthllisky farm – as a permissive path the farmer does have the right to close access, but this is unlikely! Bear right onto a farm track and continue to reach the minor road leading uphill from Porth Clais.

5. Bear left and continue to reach a crossroads. Go ahead to bear right at Clegyr Boia [5] onto a signposted bridleway and follow the track as it continues past buildings to reach a minor road. Bear left and continue on the road a short distance, bearing right onto a signposted bridleway – also sign for Felin Isaf.

6. Continue to Felin Isaf. Just past here, after a gate, there is a footpath ascending up steps – ignore and continue ahead on the bridleway through Merry Vale to reach a minor road by Glanalan. Bear right. Continue

past the houses to bear left onto the wet heath of Waun Isaf (*Lower Moor*) – cattle grid here, and signpost for St David's City walk.

7. Continue across the moor and a field to meet a path. Bear left and continue uphill to reach the access road to St Non's and Warpool Court hotel. Continue ahead and almost immediately bear left onto a path. Continue to reach residential houses. Continue ahead on Bryn Road, to bear left along Mitre Lane to reach Goat Street – the Farmers' Arms and starting point is to your left.

FACILITIES

All available in and around St David's. The cathedral has shops, café, and a gallery and treasury, where the cathedral's treasures are exhibited. The National Park's Tourist Information Centre also houses a café and an art gallery, with permanent exhibitions of the work of Graham Sutherland who worked in the county – the centre is well worth a visit just to view it's original architecture. Twr y Felin offers outdoor pursuits, and the Thousand Islands Expeditions shop exploration of the coast and the offshore islands by boat. St David's City Walk is a short leafleted National Trust walk taking in both the city and the variety of habitats to be found around the city – shop and visitor centre close to the City Cross.

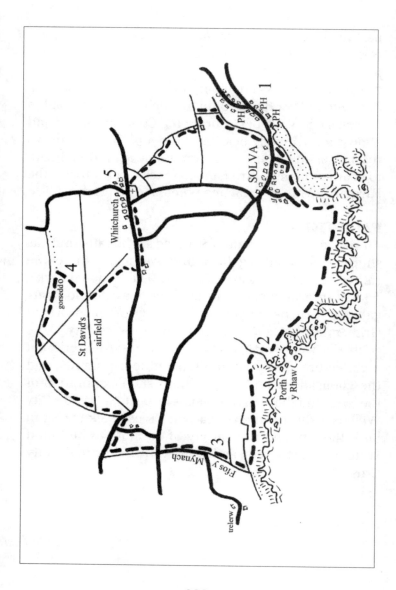

18. Solva and St David's Airfield

6.5 miles/10.5 kilometres

OS Maps: 1:25 000 North Pembrokeshire Outdoor Leisure 35.

Start: Car park in Lower Solva, in front of the Harbour Inn.

Access: Solva is 2½ miles / 4 kilometres south-east of St David's on the A487 St David's to Newgale and Haverfordwest main road. Buses 400 the Puffin Shuttle and 411 stop at Solva.

Parking: Car park in Lower Solva – seasonal charge.

Grade: Moderate.

The Cambrian Inn, Main Street, Lower Solva

(01437 721210) www.cambrianinn.co.uk

Originally a terrace of two houses and stable the inn now occupies the whole row. There may have been an ale house here in the 1600s, but in it's present form has been dated back to the 1820s. At one time it had it's own petrol pump! Plenty of local memorabilia inside. There is a garden area to the side, very colourful in summer with it's many plants and

flowers. Restaurant and bar meals, dogs welcome in the garden area. Accommodation available.

The Harbour Inn, Main Street, Lower Solva (01437 720013) www.harbourinnsolva.com
A newcomer the inn opened in the 1980s in what had been a private home as the Harbour House hotel. Garden area to front and back it's position overlooking Solva's harbour makes it a busy place during the summer months. Locally sourced food.

The Ship Inn, Main Street, Lower Solva (01437 721247)
The original Ship was sited on the other side of Main St, but in about 1815 it's then landlord moved the inn to it's present site. Internally it's exposed beams add to it's character, with one or two good model ships as befitting it's name. Good open fire for the cold days. Riverside garden to rear. Restaurant and bar meals on offer; locally sourced ales and food. Accommodation available.

HISTORY NOTES
1. Solva
Solva's harbour owes it's origins to it's history as a meltwater channel of the ice sheet that once covered the area; when sea levels rose it created a ria, a drowned valley. It's delightful setting makes it one of the most popular villages in the county. It's sheltered harbour, despite a dangerous entrance, has made it St Bride's Bay's safest port of call. There has been much speculation over the origins of the name. Those who

Solva

favour Norse origins point out that in Norse *sölv ö* can mean silver island, or *sol vo* a sunny harbour or fjord, as well as *sölva*, samphire. However the earliest references are to Salfach, closer to Solva's welsh name of Solfach.

Solva's recorded importance as a trading and commercial centre really begins in the 17th century with exports of wheat and malt, and imports of timber, cloth and oar blades. With the establishment of a shipping company in 1756 Solva entered it's period of prosperity. Unlike near neighbour Porth Clais, which could only handle vessels up to 100 tons, Solva could cater for ships of 500 tons, and by 1800 there were some thirty vessels of 20 to 250 tons here, as well as the beginnings of a shipbuilding industry. There were nine warehouses built to house corn and butter for export to particularly Bristol, though also to Ireland, and coal and limestone were brought in to fertilize the corn basket of St David's peninsula. The restored lime kilns at the head of the beach (the rectangular section being the former lime burner's hut) contributed their share of lime for the fields. Richard Fenton, Pembrokeshire's historian, describes the effect of two of Solva's former eleven kilns *whose hot vapour and dust and noise incident to them, make them very offensive, proving a great drawback on a residence on that part of the town where the chief shops and warehouses are ...* Trade had peaked by the mid 19th century, and with the coming of the railways quieter (until tourism!) and less polluted times were ahead for Solva. The last regular boat service to Bristol was finally discontinued in 1914.

Solva was host to the construction of two lighthouses for the Smalls, two notorious rocks projecting out into the Irish Sea to the west of Grassholm island's gannet colony. The first, a curious shed like affair resting on iron and oak stanchions, was constructed in the 1770s to a design by a Liverpool violin maker, Henry Whitesides. He had been the winner of a competition launched by a group of Liverpool merchants who had become frustrated at the loss of Liverpool ships on the Smalls and the reefs of the nearby Hats and Barrels. A new lighthouse of Bodmin granite was chipped and dressed on the purpose built Trinity Quay, and taken out by tug for assembly on site in 1861. Trinity Quay was home to the Solva lifeboat, the *Charles and Mary Egerton*, from 1869 until 1887, when she was sold; the St David's lifeboat being preferred.

2. Porth y Rhaw

Dating from the late first millennium BC there is a fine example here of an Iron Age fort. The large outer defensive ditch guards and gives access to three promontories, the two on the eastern side also defended by triple bank and ditch. Constructed over a number of time scales the entrance to the eastern promontory utilises a zig zag pattern, and would have offered those within a great measure of protection. There is evidence of a roundhouse within the easternmost promontory. At one time a grist mill, later a woollen mill and factory, operated from here – it's stone walls still visible by the path across the river. In operation for a hundred years or so it ceased operation in 1915.

3. Ffos y Mynach (*the Monk's Dyke*)
Running from here north to the rock outcrop of Pen Beri is the earthwork of Ffos y Mynach, in reality more a trackway. It's origins and purpose are not known, but it has the effect of enclosing St David's peninsula. As a cult site St David's may during the early Middle Ages have had a large enclosure built around it, and such enclosures did confer rights of sanctuary. Still traceable at Dowrog Common and at Pen Beri it makes for a walk of five miles / eight kilometres. Combine with the Coast Path for a day's walk of some twenty miles / thirty kilometres!

4. St David's airfield
Pembrokeshire's coastal position offered a prime location for aircraft involved in the Second World War Battle of the Atlantic, maritime trade needed protection and the German U-boats constant surveillance. Between 1939 and 1945 eight airfields were constructed in the county, St David's the last in 1943. It had been intended for United States Navy Liberator bombers, but change of

plans led to use by the RAF's Flying Fortress bombers, and then by Halifax bombers, these in their turn succeeded by Liberators. The classic wartime layout of three runways laid out in a triangular pattern was used here, and can still be traced, but of the control tower, hangars and ancillary buildings little remains. Nearby RAF Brawdy was opened in 1944 as a satellite station for St David's, but later it became the senior airfield. The RAF withdrew from Brawdy in 1992 and it is now home to the Royal Signals. From 1974 to 1995 the United States operated a base adjacent to Brawdy, which formed part of it's international undersea surveillance system. St David's itself continued in use, for a number of years it had a fleet support role, but activity ceased by 1960, though from 1974 to 1992 one of it's runways acted as a relief landing area for RAF Brawdy. St David's airfield was declared surplus in the 1980s and was acquired by the National Park in 1996. Reversion to heathland is being encouraged, and it is now an important site for breeding skylarks, it's grassland managed as an organic hay meadow.

5. Whitchurch

An attractive village it's Welsh name is Tregroes, in English *Settlement of the Cross*. It takes it's Welsh name from a small standing stone known as Maen Dewi, St David's stone. This Celtic style church is dedicated to St David – it's nave, chancel, and it's north transept with it's squint are probably late 13th century. The church was restored in 1874. Whitchurch gives it's name to the parish which includes Solva, and it's church is the parish church.

WALK DIRECTIONS [-] indicates history note

1. Starting from the car park in front of the Harbour Inn in Lower Solva [1] go along the path to the right of the inlet and continue to the Solva Boat Club building. Continue ahead on the Coast Path as it ascends through houses to the coast.

2. The Path passes through the bay and Iron Age fort of Porth y Rhaw [2]. Continue ahead on the Coast Path from here for ½ mile / ¾ kilometre or so. Whilst the Coast Path continues ahead the route bears right inland − look for a large signpost with a walking man directing you to a walker's gate giving entrance to a field. This is the beginning (or end) of the Ffos y Mynach [3].

3. Continue across two fields, keeping by the hedge on the left, to reach a minor road. Continue ahead to reach the main A road to St David's. Cross and go directly ahead on a bridleway to meet another minor road. Bear right and continue ahead to reach on the left one of the entrances to St David's airfield [4].

4. Go ahead through the gate and follow the path along the old runway − there is an earthbank that runs along the route, and whilst it is possible to walk either side keeping the bank to the right gives better views over St David's peninsula to the left. Continue to reach a Gorsedd stone circle on your right − the circle commemorates the National Eisteddfod of Wales, held here 2002. Just past the circle bear right onto a well marked path − at the path crossroads continue ahead to reach a minor road.

5. At the minor road bear left and continue to reach Whitchurch [5] and it's church. Just past the church

cross a stile into a field and bear diagonally left to reach a stile on top of the hedgebank. Cross and keeping the hedge to your left continue across three fields to reach a road by a house. Cross the stile and bear left.

6. At a cattle grid bear right into another field, and keeping to the right reach a metal gate giving access to a path above the valley below. Bear right and stay on this path as it leads back to Solva. Take the steps down to Quarry Cottage to reach the main road through Solva opposite the road of Penyraber. Bear left downhill on the pavement, to shortly bear right on the road giving vehicular access to Solva Boat Club. Once back at the path alongside the inlet bear left to return to the starting point.

FACILITIES

Most available in Solva. Those wishing to head uphill to explore Upper Solva will find the Royal George offering bar meals and views over Solva's harbour and the coast.